A GENTLEMAN'S DAUGHTER:

The life of Harriet Mary Dowling (née Blaxland) in

India and Australia in colonial times

By Alison Ferguson

Copyright © Alison Ferguson 2017

All rights reserved. No part of this book may be reproduced or transmitted in any form or by any means, electronic or mechanical, including photocopying, recording or by any information storage and retrieval system, without prior permission in writing from the author. The *Australian Copyright Act 1968* (the Act) allows a maximum of one chapter or 10 per cent of this book, whichever is the greater, to be photocopied by any educational institution for its educational purposes provided that the educational institution (or body that administers it) has given a remuneration notice to the Copyright Agency (Australia) under the Act.

Backstory Press

Email:backstorypress@gmail.com
Web: www.backstorypress.com

ISBN-978-0-9876227-0-9

Set in 11/12 pt Baskerville Old, 14 pt Book Antiqua

Cover illustration:

Botanical drawing around1879, by Anna Frances Walker (1830-1913) Image freely available to publish without permission from the collections of the State Library of NSW, Catalogue V/72.

Correction:
The previous version of this book contained an image (described as Harriet Dowling at around 60 year of age) which was in fact her niece, Harriott Mary Norton nee Walker. My heartfelt thanks to the reader who alerted me to this error. The image has been removed in the present version.

Dedication

In memory of Gordon King,

who introduced me to Harriet

Contents

1	INTRODUCTION	1
2	PENAL PRIVILEGE	2
3	THE BOTANY BAY FLOWER	16
4	A VIEW OF THE RUINS	26
5	THE FRENCH COMMODORE	33
6	DESTITUTION	39
7	DOCTOR RITCHIE	44
8	THE SECOND LADY IN THE COLONY	55
9	FORGIVENESS	64
10	HOME IS A FIRST-CLASS CABIN	68
11	A SHARED INDULGENCE	79
APPENDICES		80
ACKNOWLEDGEMENTS		85
BIBLIOGRAPHY		87
WORKS CITED		101
INDEX		112

List of illustrations

1. George Street, Sydney in 1829 4
2. Rebellion on 26 January 1808 6
3. Parramatta 1809 9
4. Budgerow 18
5. Shopping in Kolkata (for the British) 22
6. St John's Church, Kolkata 24
7. Marriage Register at St John's Church, 1816 25
8. Taj Mahal in early 1800s 30
9. Baron Hyacinthe de Bougainville 35
10. Meeting the Pilot Boat at Sand Heads 39
11. First Agricultural Fair in Parramatta, 1823 44
12. Newington House, Parramatta 46
13. John Blaxland in 1832 47
14. Baron Charles von Hügel 52
15. Jane Blaxland in around 1835 53
16. St John's Church, Parramatta 54
17. Brougham Lodge, Darlinghurst in 1848 56
18. Sir James Dowling in 1840 59
19. Harriet de Marquet Blaxland 71
20. Harriet Dowling's passport, 1858 74

List of Appendices

Appendix 1 Harriet and her brothers and sisters 80
Appendix 2 Harriet's relatives from India 81
Appendix 3 Harriet's Children 82
Appendix 4 Harriet's Step-Children 83
Appendix 5 Summary of Events in Harriet's life 84

Preliminaries

I've provided a listing of footnoted sources in the 'Works Cited' section, and a Bibliography at the end of the book. Where I have quoted multiple passages from a single source, I have footnoted the material on the first occasion and then relied on the text to indicate the authorship of subsequent passages. Where I have quoted an excerpt from source material, I have used double quotes ("...") through the text. I have used single quotes ('...') for quotes within quotes and to characterise particular terms.

Nineteenth century spelling was variable so, for example, Harriet spelled her own name in different ways at different times as did her mother (also named Harriet). When quoting, I have maintained spelling as used in original documents. However, in the text, I have used the current spelling for names of people and places: for example, 'Kolkata' for 'Calcutta', 'Hugli River' for 'Hooghly River'.

For currency conversions, I have used the methods and conversion tables at MeasuringWorth.com, which provides data up to 2015; with UK data from 1207 and Australian data from 1828. When estimating the worth of estates, loans and wages, I have used the index of per capita GDP, and for estimating affordability, I have used the index of the GDP deflator.

1 Introduction

When I came across the unpublished "Memoir of the early life of Harriet Mary Dowling nee Blaxland (1799-1881): Or sketches of India and Australia in old times",[1] I had my usual cynical reaction. To my way of thinking, memoirs were a land grab on the future real estate of the historical property market. Memoirists wrote from an inflated sense of the value of their life to others; past, present, and future.

When the memoirist seeks to take a selfie of their life, then the way they photo-shop that image can paint a far more interesting picture for the reader than the content itself. Which angles do they choose and which blemishes do they seek to airbrush? I was fascinated with the way Harriet's character emerged from what she chose to highlight in her tales and from the matters she chose to ignore, both about herself and the social milieu which surrounded her.

So it was that I came to be entranced by Harriet, to be captivated by her vanities, to be astonished by her self-focus, and to be grateful for her illumination of a woman's options in colonial New South Wales and India in the first half of the nineteenth century.

Harriet's story teases the imagination and so I've wandered into some informed speculation. From what I've learned about Harriet, I don't think she would have minded.

2 Penal Privilege

Harriet sailed to the barely functional colony of Sydney at the age of six as the eldest daughter of John Blaxland (1769–1845) and Harriet Mary de Marquet Blaxland (1777–1852). The year was 1806 and, after eighteen years, the British penal settlement was still struggling to feed itself and the British government had begun encouraging the migration of free settlers.

For Harriet, all that mattered was the adventure: "My early memories of the colony I may say commenced with the journey of fifteen miles from Sydney to Parramatta in the only carriage of those days, a 'gig' lent as a particular favour. Seated as I was on a cushion between my Father's knees, not a bridge had then been built with three rivers to cross, which could only be effected at low tide by getting out of the gig and stepping from stone to stone. The road—a cart track—only the width of the wheels, the wild natural forest almost closing overhead, chill and silent as it was can never be forgotten."

The journey to the family's property was exciting, not only because of the rivers to cross but also because of her pride of place in the gig with her father. Harriet's mother was pregnant with Louisa Australia Blaxland so she and the rest of the family and their goods were conveyed in more substantial conveyances by road and river.

As a child, Harriet had no awareness of the immensity of the family's migration to the other side of the world: from a life where the social order had been entrenched for centuries to a place where it wasn't just the seasons that were upside-down.

Her parents were not by nature adventurers. They had deliberated long and hard before making the decision to move. The economic indicators in England, despite the lull in the Napoleonic Wars, were not propitious and the Blaxlands had weighed up the family's prospects if they maintained their farmland in Kent or migrated to one of the colonies. Canada was considered at one point, but the flattering assurances made by Sir Joseph Banks and the promises of government support induced the family to sell up and migrate to New South Wales.

The youngest Blaxland brother, Gregory, made the journey a year earlier with his family at government expense in the convict ship, the *William Pitt*. On his arrival, Governor King provided 4,000 acres of land, convict labour (10 per 1,000 acres to be supplied as needed) and stock (80 cows in return for additional payment) in line with instructions from Viscount Castlereagh, the Secretary of State for War and the Colonies.[2]

Harriet's father had expectations of even more substantial assistance from the government.[3] He had established an agreement with Viscount Castlereagh that, in return for £6,000 (currently equivalent to $AUD 16 million, about one-third of the sale of Blaxland properties in Kent), he would receive land grants totalling 8,000 acres and 80 convicts (expenses for their food and clothing to be borne by the government for eighteen months) as well as stock (for additional payment). After finalising the sale of their estates in Kent, he made the journey at his own expense in the ship *The Brothers*, in which he and Gregory had purchased a share with Hullet Brothers & Company of London.

The town centre of Sydney was the commercial hub and John purchased the lease from Joseph Fleming for a property at the corner of Market Street and George Street (then known as High Street) which became the site of the brothers' saleyards and butchery.

1 GEORGE STREET, SYDNEY IN 1829

"George Street from the Wharf, Select Views of Sydney New South Wales 1829." Drawn and engraved by John Carmichael, Sydney. Image from the collections of the State Library of NSW, Catalogue PXB 359/No.3 (freely available to publish without permission).

The Blaxland brothers' land grants were closer to Parramatta where the early seat of government was established. Gregory Blaxland settled his family estate at Brush Farm in what is now the suburb of Ryde. John Blaxland's property was across the other side of the Parramatta River at Newington Farm (named after the family estate in Kent)—now the suburb of Silverwater.

Rebellion

By the time Harriet's family had arrived, Governor King had been replaced by Governor Bligh. The new Governor lived up to his *Bounty* reputation as a martinet[4] and was not as obliging as his predecessor in relation to fulfilling the assurances of support that John Blaxland had received. Initially, relations with Governor Bligh were cordial, at least as far as Bligh was concerned since he reported that when they arrived: "I had them every day with us and gave a public dinner to introduce Mrs Blaxland to all the ladies of the colony."[5]

However, Governor Bligh took a dim view of what he saw as the Blaxland brothers' speculative enterprises, which included the seal trade and an application for a distillery.[6] He also frowned upon their business dealings with the ex-convict, Simeon Lord.[7] Although the Newington land grant of 1,290 acres was provided in 1807, Bligh provided less support than had been promised by the government.

The control of the convict colony was through direct military rule of the Governor. John Blaxland had seen military service, as a captain in the Duke of York's Cavalry.[8] However, for men such as the Blaxlands, life as gentlemen farmers of substance had imbued them with a strong sense of their rights.[9] Also, for the Blaxlands, long-lasting grievance was coded in their DNA. They were proud of their ancestry which dated back before the Norman Conquest and still talked of the family holdings on the Ilse of Thanet as being "wrested" from the family back in 1066.[10,11] Their social aspirations aligned them with the ruling class, although their identification as 'Men of Kent' carried the connotation of independence in the face of authority, due to the historical tradition that men from East Kent did not surrender to William the Conqueror.[12]

As well as the Blaxland brothers being a thorn in his side, Governor Bligh's authority was challenged by increasing demands of ex-military land owners (such as John Macarthur) and the growing number of entrepreneurial emancipists such as Simeon Lord. Infuriated by Bligh's failure to recognise what they saw as their entitlements, the Blaxlands supported the rebellion of 26th January 1808 against Bligh. Both brothers signed the petition seeking the army corps to take over control of the colony, with John signing his name directly under the ringleader, John Macarthur.[13]

2 REBELLION ON 26 JANUARY 1808

"*Major Johnson announcing the arrest of Governor Bligh.*" Copy of 1928 painting by Raymond Lindsay (public domain, https://historymatrix.wordpress.com/tag/rum-rebellion).

After Bligh was deposed, John lobbied Major Johnston of the New South Wales army corps to meet his requirements. When this also failed to achieve the expected support, John set out in September 1808 to England to press his claims. His departure was a bare eighteen months after his arrival in the colony. On the way to England, John was arrested and gaoled (without charge) on Bligh's instructions in Cape Town. He eventually reached England but was required to stay as a witness in Johnston's court martial.[14]

Harriet's world

When John Blaxland left for England, he left his wife to run a new estate in a new country, with his brother's assistance. She was pregnant once more (this time with Eliza Maria, born December 1808) and managing five children under the age of eight: eight-year-old Harriet Mary, six-year-old John Marquet, five-year-old George, three-year-old Anna Elizabeth, two-year-old Jane Elizabeth, and one-year-old Louisa Australia. At some point during his absence, young John and George were sent to England to join their father, since he mentions that his two sons would need to accompany him back to the colony in his 'memorial' of 1811 to the Earl of Liverpool (Secretary of State for War and the Colonies at that time) seeking financial compensation. (See the Appendices for a full list of the Blaxland children.)

Harriet spent this part of her childhood assisting with the care of her younger brothers and sisters. However, her mother's situation meant that, in some ways, the children were at more liberty than their peers back in England. They spent much of their day out of doors—horse-riding and rambling in the search for native flora to collect. As had occurred back in Kent, Harriet mixed with her brothers and sisters and cousins, who were of similar ages. Beyond the family, they socialised with the small number of people of a similar social status.

However, their lives in their new country had changed due to the role played by convict labour both on the estate and within the household.[15] For the Blaxlands, like all free settlers, convict labour was essential in establishing farm land and stock management and, with government stores supporting their provisions, convicts came at minimal cost. In New South Wales in 1806,[16] there were 2,223 convicts and 1,938 ex-convicts who between them made up 85% of the population. The colony also had a growing young population of 807 legitimate children and 988 illegitimate children. Convict servants staffed the settlers' households as did the children of convicts from the Orphan School (originally established by Governor King in 1801 in George Street and relocated to Parramatta in 1823).[17] The upstairs-downstairs divide of the mother country persisted in this raw settlement of single storeyed homes.[18] Harriet would later refer to the colony's "badge of disgrace": an attitude which would prevail amongst the community for another century.

Even more invisible in Harriet's account was the local aboriginal population. The Dharug and Gadigal peoples populated the area around Sydney and Parramatta[19] where Harriet grew up. It was their land upon which the Blaxlands established themselves, but Harriet recorded no memory of them. Harriet's world in the new colony was isolated, protected, and privileged.

3 PARRAMATTA 1809

"A view of part of Parramatta, Port Jackson, 1809."
Watercolour by J.W. Lewin, in *Series 01: Australian paintings* by J.W. Lewin, G.P. Harris, G.W. Evans and others, 1796-1809. Image from the collections of the State Library of NSW, Catalogue PXB 388 Volume 3, f.6 (freely available to publish without permission).

Father and daughter

Harriet's life changed with the return of her father from England after his four-year absence. When he had left, she had been a child of eight but, when she saw him again, she was a pre-pubescent twelve-year-old. John Blaxland had always been a serious man and, no doubt, had always been a strict father. However, Harriet's childhood memory of their shared ride in the gig out to Parramatta conveyed a sense of security in her father's indulgence. By the time of his return, his experiences during his four years' absence had hardened the more rigid aspects of his character as a man and as a parent.

Within weeks of leaving the colony, he had gone from being a man of some consequence to being a prisoner in Cape Town. The three months of his imprisonment were grim.[20] Following his arrest, he was incarcerated in a "noisome" Dutch gaol, where he caught gaol fever which continued to affect him long afterward. Next, he was moved to confinement on a British ship down in the cockpit (at the stern where midshipmen berthed). Eventually, he was relocated to one of the officers' cabins in the gun-room. Physical hardship aside, what festered in John's heart was the injustice. He had been imprisoned without charge at the request of a man he considered to have been lawfully deposed and therefore, lacking any authority. Further, he had been exposed to public shame amongst his countrymen by his arrival back in England as a prisoner. Although John had only spent eighteen months in a penal colony, that time would have been sufficient to sharpen his sense of the shame and ignominy of imprisonment. Adding insult to injury, he was released without any charges having been laid and the matter was essentially made to disappear.

For all his familial culture of complaint, when John had left England he had been a confident man, hopeful of the future. By his return, his cautious optimism had soured. He had extended his outrage to include Sir Joseph Banks, who Harriet later described as having "inveigled" the Blaxland brothers through his encouragement of their decision to move. John's disputes continued with each successive governor of the colony. Also, he was unhappy with the decisions that Gregory had made in his absence[21] and their business partnership was dissolved in 1813.[22] John Blaxland felt that his wife had been persuaded to accept less-than-adequate government support by Bligh's replacement,

Governor Macquarie. John's pastoral focus on cattle (including meat and salt works) ran counter to the agricultural priorities of the Governor and it was not until 1813 that Macquarie finalised the major land grant of 6,710 acres between the Nepean River and South Creek, which John named Luddenham.[23]

John Blaxland's heightened awareness of the thin divide between shame and respectability made him an unforgiving and controlling father. His long absence could explain Harriet's frustration when under his authority from that point onward.

Apollo

Harriet's dissatisfaction with her life was partly pre-adolescent angst and partly boredom. With women in short supply in the colony, governesses proved almost impossible to keep, so Harriet's education was in the hands of her mother. The prevailing norms for a girl's education focused on basic literacy, arithmetic, religion and sewing—with the addition of accomplishments such as music, art, and French for those with societal aspirations.[24,25] Harriet's sisters—Jane, Louisa and Anna—were skilful in drawing and were encouraged by their mother to develop their botanical knowledge by collecting local plants and flowers.[26] Their mother's father had been French, so it was likely that their mother spoke French fluently and that she had a hand in ensuring that her daughters acquired similar skill. However, Harriet described her main occupation as acting as a "nurse-maid" with considerable irritation.

Harriet's boredom lifted on meeting the handsome Captain Cowin: "...the destiny of my life was cast on seeing for the first time an 'Apollo'...at the first glance of this perfection of manly beauty clad in a bright full uniform, my sight left me. At the moment I had a tray in my hands with cake and wine offering to my mother's old friends just arrived from England. A sudden shake of the shoulder from my mother to save her glasses—which were falling—recalled my senses, and with burning cheeks I rushed away. From that hour I was miserably in love—useless to myself and taking interest in nothing that I ought and Captain Cowin treating me as a child, as I really was."

Harriet was right in recalling that she thought about nothing else than the handsome Captain. Her father's return barely rated a mention in her memoir and she completely failed to note that her Uncle Gregory had, with William Lawson and William Charles Wentworth, succeeded in finding a way across the Blue Mountains in May, 1813.[27] Captain Cowin was in the 73rd (Perthshire) Regiment, an infantry regiment of the British Army, also known as MacLeod's Highlanders.[28] Between 1810 and 1814, the 1st Battalion were stationed in New South Wales but shortly after Harriet had met him, the regiment left for India and Ceylon (Sri Lanka) in 1814 to fight in the 2nd Kandyan War. With her Apollo's departure, Harriet thought longingly of life in India.

Harriet's relatives in India

Harriet's mother had been born in India and told exciting tales of Harriet's grandmother's life.[29] Harriet's mother's half-sister, Elizabeth Hogue, had returned to live in India and the relationship between the two half-sisters was to play a large part in Harriet's life (a diagram of Harriet's relatives from India is provided in the Appendices).

Harriet's grandmother (Elizabeth Carter) had been adopted by Colonel White and his wife when she was young (although her parents, farmers, were alive). As Colonel White was an aide-de-camp of Warren Hastings—Governor-General of Bengal between 1773 and 1785—she moved with the Whites to India at the age of five. She married a French merchant, whose status grew over the course of the family history. Harriet's mother described him as "John Marquet, a merchant...of the De Marquets of Dauphiné"[30] while, in generations to come, he was described as, "Count Louis de Marquet of Monaco, Councillor of the King Frances of the nation, and an officer of the Bodyguard of Louis XV."[31] In 1777, Harriet's mother, Harriet de Marquet, was born in India and she told Harriet about a childhood playing in the "Palace" (Government House).

Following the early death of her father, Harriet de Marquet was sent to England at the age of five to live in the care of friends. Her mother (Elizabeth de Marquet, née Carter) stayed in India and later married Marquet's business partner, Mr Andrews. They had a daughter, Elizabeth (half-sister to Harriet de Marquet) and moved back to England. From the age of fourteen, Harriet de Marquet lived with the Andrews at Barrow House in Somersetshire until her marriage.

In 1797, when she was twenty-two, Harriet de Marquet married John Blaxland, a twenty-nine-year-old widower, whose first wife (Sarah Davies) had died in childbirth two years before. Her half-sister, Elizabeth Andrews, returned to India after she married Arthur Hogue who was the wealthy senior partner of an agency for the East India Company—Hogue, Davidson and Robertson.

The invitation to India

While Harriet was still dreaming about the glamorous Captain and the excitements of India, Aunt Hogue wrote to the Blaxlands to invite Harriet and her brother, George to live with her family in Kolkata. The invitation might have been prompted by some feeling of obligation on the part of the Hogues, due to a financial dispute between the two half-sisters—Harriet de Marquet Blaxland and Elizabeth Andrews Hogue— regarding their mother's estate.

Their mother left her estate to Mr Andrews as a life tenant through a Trust Deed.[32] On his death in 1810, the estate was left to Elizabeth Hogue but the Blaxlands argued that they were entitled to a share. As well as providing patronage of Harriet and George while they were in India, Uncle Hogue later helped to finance developments at Newington, New South Wales. He held a mortgage on the Newington property, with the title deeds not released to John Blaxland until 29th April 1828. Even at that time, John still owed Hogue £1,000 (currently equivalent to over $AUD 1 million). This matter would prove to have repercussions for Harriet across her life.

The argument for Harriet to move to Kolkata was that the wider society would provide her with the opportunity to finish her education, i.e., nineteenth century code for a social curriculum of dancing and match-making. Harriet wrote: "The astonishment of my father and mother that I could leave them was great indeed. They knew nothing of my secret hope of again meeting Captain Cowin in Calcutta."

For the naïve Harriet, travelling to India was about discarding parental control for love and romance. However, she failed to grasp the essentials of husband-hunting for the nineteenth century woman: money and position in society.

On Monday 1st August 1814,[33] fourteen-year-old Harriet and eleven-year-old George set out on the three-month voyage to Kolkata on the *Eliza*, one of the Hogues' thirty-six ships.

"The Asiatic Mirror, mentioning the arrival at Bengal of the Eliza, Capt Murray, on the 3rd of November last, states as follows: On her passage from New South Wales, the Eliza fell in with the brig Hibernia, Capt Ashmore, of Calcutta, and the schooner Derwent, Capt Carr; parted from them on the 1st September in sight of Boobie Island. While in company with the Hibernia, passing through Torres's straits, the Eliza saw the wreck of the brig Morning Star (late of Calcutta), Capt Smart, from Port Jackson, bound to Batavia. On the 30th September the Eliza observed a white flag flying on Boobie Island, where she sent a boat on shore, and there found five of the crew of the Morning Star, which Capt Murray had brought back to Calcutta. Capt Smart, with nine of his crew had five days previously left the island in the brig's longboat for Timor. The following passengers have arrived here on the Eliza: Mrs. Murray and child, Master George; and Miss Harriett Blaxland."

The Sydney Gazette and New South Wales Advertiser, Wednesday 19 April, 1815, page 2.[34]

---

3   The Botany Bay Flower

Harriet's memory of the voyage to Kolkata in the *Eliza* was vivid: "In the passage of three days through the Straits the scenery was beautiful, resembling a vast lake studded with islands of the most varied and brilliant tints of green, thickly wooded with palm and cocoa-nut trees meeting the water's edge. Sleeping turtles of immense size passing by and knots of huge sea-snakes, in colour and marked like tortoise shell, linked together in the centre and spread out like a wheel quite six feet in diameter, disgusting to look at, said not to be venomous."

In her concentration on the wildlife in Torres Strait, she neglected to mention the *Eliza*'s role in rescuing the five shipwrecked sailors from another of the Hogue's ships, *The Morning Star* from Boobie Island.[35]

Harriet's memory of this rescue may have been overshadowed by the traumatic events that followed, when the Captain's pregnant wife (brought along to chaperone Harriet) went into labour and her Indian servant went into hiding. "Then came Captain Murray, entreating me to go to his poor wife, a lady of forty years of age, half of which time she had been engaged to her husband and had never left the Isle of Skye till she was married. What a position for a young girl, brought up as I had been? Nevertheless, I was better than none, and after overcoming my horror, my necessary directions gladly made myself useful, though sinking at times and almost fainting in my intense alarm. When all was over and a daughter born the ayah returned to her duties, but I still was the chief nurse the few days we were passing up the Hooghly."

Harriet's brother Edward had been born a year before she left for Kolkata. Considering the family's standing in the colony, her mother might have been attended by both a doctor and midwife. On the other hand, finding servants was difficult and Harriet described her role as "nurse-maid", so she might have been present for Edward's birth. Also, Newington Farm would have involved animal husbandry associated with the Blaxland's cattle interests. This exposure to rural life meant that Harriet would have had opportunities to see animals giving birth. Regardless of any of this potential experience, her situation at fourteen years of age as the sole responsible female to assist the birth of a first child to an older mother would have been frightening, and there was a note of pride in her recollection of the successful outcome.

To approach Kolkata, ships needed to be piloted through the shifting sand banks of Sand Heads at the mouth of the Hugli River (formerly the Hooghly River). Larger vessels docked 140 kilometres further up the river at Diamond Harbour, while smaller craft could proceed another 50 kilometres to Kolkata. Harriet and George were met by Uncle Hogue and travelled up the Hugli River by budgerow (a long flat-bottomed barge, some with cabins). Her excitement peaked as they approached: "As night closed in I alone remained awake watching the new and strange objects in rapid succession passing....The clusters of tall elegant waving bamboos almost meeting the water along the banks were thickly studded with fire flies, most brilliant. Not having heard of them, I looked upon these moving objects as something supernatural, yet dare not wake my uncle to ask."

4 BUDGEROW

Image is from late 18th century, artist F.B. Solvyns (1760-1824), from "*Manners, customs and dresses of the Hindoos*" published in 1798 (located in Victoria and Albert Museum, public domain).

The budgerow took them to Chandpal Ghat—a landing place with terraced steps into the water—in the centre of the British part of Kolkata. They were taken from there in palanquins (litters). Harriet's palanquin was a seated sedan chair but George had the misfortune to travel in one with a slung hammock suspended from poles carried by bearers, and found himself tipped out onto the ground. The trip in the palanquin would not have been a long one as Hastings Street was about a block away from the ghat. The house was centrally located near Esplanade Row (East) and Old Courthouse Street (now Sidhu Kanu Dahar), and opposite St John's Church.

Harriet fell in love with her rich surroundings. Her description of her first impressions evoked the atmosphere of the popular novels[36,37] that she would have read: "...I was shown to my room upstairs by a figure swathed from head to feet in white muslin. I thought of a ghost yet followed as I was told—this was an ayah intended for me. In passing through the drawing-room with rows of marble columns here and there, figures appeared in white, all looking stealthily at me. I must say at last I became nervous. On returning to the dining hall, a blaze of light with a vast machine waving fan-like over the table between double rows of vast white marble columns...the hall with black and white marble floor was thirty feet long covered with a Turkey carpet. My bewilderment can be imagined but not expressed. The number of men in attendance, each in white muslin, with silver crests in their turbans was another astonishment, but I understood it better on hearing the full establishment consisted of a hundred domestics."

Harriet described her uncle as a genial gentleman who dressed for comfort rather than fashion: "Never before had I seen such a dress as his, anything but what I expected—nankeen shorts with silver knee buckles, white ribbed silk stockings, buckles in shoes, cut and slashed across the toes to give ease to many corns which were troublesome."

She developed a great affection for Uncle Hogue, but not so for her aunt who "cared but little for society, her children and heaps of books absorbing every thought and may I add feeling. I was left entirely to my kind uncle in comparison to my aunt's neglect till at last he took me about with him wherever he went." Aunt Elizabeth Hogue had given birth to three children in the three years preceding Harriet's arrival and bore another child again the next year. It was not surprising, then, that she was preoccupied with concerns other than paying attention to adolescent Harriet.

India for Harriet was both familiar and exotic. During this period, India had a small British population—estimated to be around 45,000 out of 150 million for the total population.[38] This population was dominated by men, as the East India Company did not encourage the bringing of wives and families to India. Harriet found that her dancing lessons were about a block away in Old Government House (now Raj Bhawan) where her mother had visited as a child. As a member of British society in Kolkata, Harriet was taken for the daily afternoon drive around "The Course" (her description for what later became a racecourse in part of the large parkland space around Fort William known as the Maidan). This carriage ride and her dancing provided her only exercise and contrasted with the physical freedom she had known in Sydney.[39] Her childhood, spent outdoors under the Australian sun, was evident by her complexion. "My bright colour on arrival gave great offence, being considered extremely vulgar, and my natural flow of spirits was equally condemned. At this time so little was understood of Australia that I became quite a curiosity and better known as 'The Botany Bay Flower'."

Her contact with the Indian population was restricted to particular classes. All matters to do with the household management and her personal care were mediated through the many servants employed by the Hogues, each operating within the scope and constraints dictated by the caste system.

At the other end of the social spectrum, she met the impressive Rajah Ram Mohan Roy (who went on to found the influential socio-religious reform movement known as the Brahmo Samaj). Apparently, she impressed the Rajah, as family stories told of his comment that Harriet looked as though she had "fallen from heaven" and was the loveliest "houri" (beautiful young virgin) he had ever seen.

As she accompanied her uncle going about his business, she also met wealthy Indian 'baboos' (babu)—the nouveau-riche intermediaries in trade between the two cultures.[40] "At times the display of jewels was dazzling, placed always upon large trays covered with scarlet velvet with deep gold fringes. These were taken around to be seen and admired. The greatest display I ever saw of this sort was upon the marriage of the eldest son of one of these merchants. The bridegroom, a youth of perhaps sixteen, the perfection of Asiatic beauty, appeared literally covered with magnificent pearls and diamonds of great value."

Going about with Uncle Hogue and attending dancing lessons could occupy only so much of her day and, within a year, she also lost the companionship of her brother, George. Uncle Hogue arranged for George to join the Bombay Marine (owned by the East India Company, and operating as a de facto arm of the British navy). However, George was deeply unhappy in the Marine and, through the ever-kind offices of Uncle Hogue, he managed to quit the Marine to join the merchant navy associated with the firm of Hogue, Davidson and Robertson, involved in trade between India and the Guangzhou region in south-eastern China (formerly Canton). Operating out of China, Davidson & Co later became Dent & Co, one of the British merchant houses known as the 'Hongs'.

A Gentleman's Daughter

5 SHOPPING IN KOLKATA (FOR THE BRITISH)

Illustration of Taylor & Co's emporium, drawn for "*Tom Raw, the griffin*" by Charles D'Oyly, 1828, but not used (Creative Commons CC0 1.0 Universal Public Domain Dedication).

Harriet, much to the disapproval of her aunt and uncle, spent an increasing amount of time with Alexander Macdonald, one of the many writers' clerks who lived with the Hogues at their Hastings Street home. Writers' clerks were employed by the East India Company to manage the records of the vast number of commercial transactions of the widely disseminated business. Alexander ("Sandy" as Harriet referred to him), was a nephew of the Hogues (probably of Uncle Hogue). She described him as "...six feet in height, admirably proportioned in form, good looking but nothing remarkable, with a full rich voice and sang to perfection old Scotch songs."

He had no money and an obscure background. His only asset was the patronage of Uncle Hogue. Harriet's description of his good points, though complimentary in essence, was hardly glowing. However, Harriet went on to lobby hard for permission to marry him, so what possessed her?

She had at least one alternative suitor: "I was sought for in marriage by one of the oldest civilians celebrated for his wealth, Mr B. Martin, possessing £1,000,000 sterling" (currently equivalent to over $AUD 2 billion). She accounted for her actions in the following way: "...in age about 60, head bald as an ostrich egg surrounded by a fringe of white hair tied at the back in a cue with black ribbon...Such was my admirer!!! What else could I do but laugh? Nevertheless, he was in earnest and did his best to obtain me from my uncle, but gold was never my God. Several others followed and seeing my uncle seriously annoyed I sought advice from Sandy, who soon made proposals himself, and I gladly accepted his offer to be released from so much worry."

Harriet's resilience under family pressure up to that point was demonstrably strong, so the suggestion that she married him to avoid "worry" was unlikely. Also, for a person for whom "gold was never her God" she spent a striking amount of energy in describing her memories of riches. In terms of fortune, Sandy was an unwise choice and, from her description of him, she appeared to be anything but swept off her feet. A suspicious mind might turn to consider the birth date of their first child. However, this would lead to disappointment, as their daughter Elizabeth (Eliza) Ritchie was born a respectable twelve months later. Whatever the reason, over the eighteen months she had been in Kolkata, they had forged a friendship, and the nature of the marriage that followed seemed to reflect that this continued.

The Hogues, as her guardians, were persuaded to agree to the marriage. Uncle Hogue went further—he gave Sandy a lac (now 'lakh') of rupees (100,000) at a time when European wages in India were about 100-200 rupees a month. He also made Sandy a junior partner of the firm and built an apartment for the couple within the new house he had constructed for the family over the other side of the river in Shibpur. In return, he took the liberty, with a wry sense of humour, of adding "Ritchie" to Sandy's name so that he became Alexander Macdonald Ritchie.

Harriet and Ritchie were married in St John's Church in what Harriet described as "an exceedingly quiet wedding" on 3rd June 1816. She was sixteen.

6 St John's Church, Kolkata

"*View of St John's cathedral Calcutta, 1826.*" Painted by James Baillie Fraser (original held in British Library, public domain).

A Gentleman's Daughter

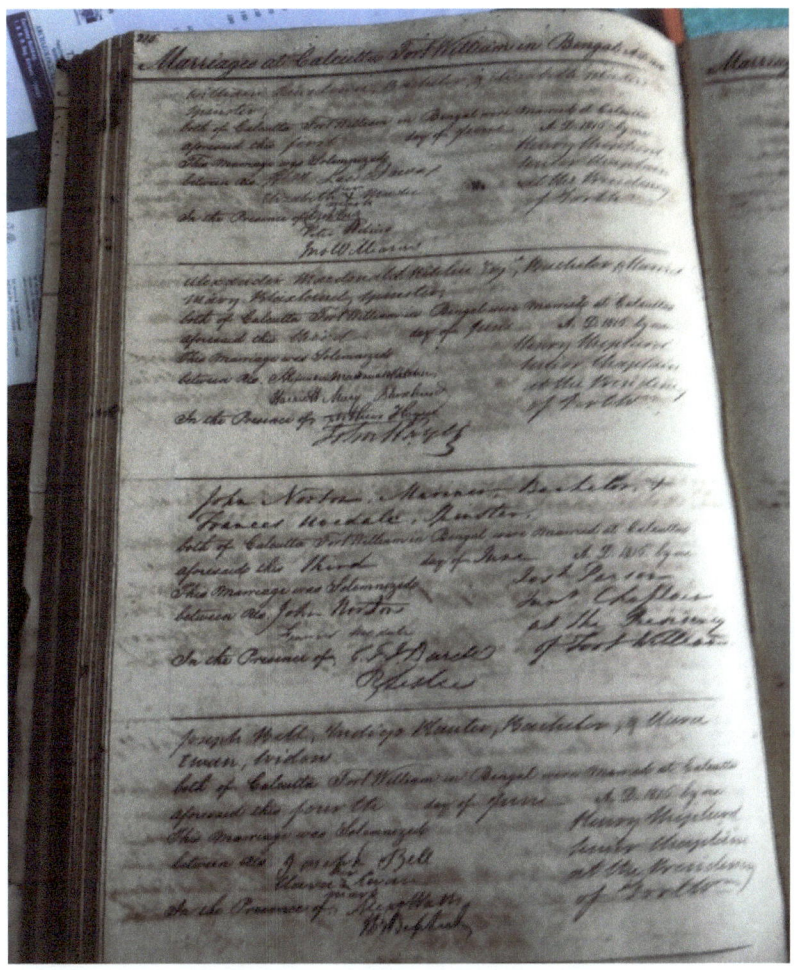

7 MARRIAGE REGISTER AT ST JOHN'S CHURCH, 1816

Text (second entry on page) reads: "*Alexander Macdonald Ritchie Esq, Bachelor, and Harriet Mary Blaxland, Spinster, both of Calcutta Fort William in Bengal were married at Calcutta aforesaid this third day of June, AD 1816, by me. Henry Shepherd, Senior Chaplain at the Residency of Fort William. This marriage was solemnized between Alexander Macdonald Ritchie, Harriett Mary Blaxland, In the Presence of Arthur Hogue, John Hayes*" (photographed by the author, with permission).

4 A View of the Ruins

The first year of Harriet's life as Mrs Ritchie was idyllic. For their ten-day honeymoon, they sailed up the Hugli River to visit the historic towns established by other colonial powers: Chuchura (Dutch Chinsurah), Chandannagar (French Chandanagore), and Srerampur (Danish Serampore). Their apartment consisted of four rooms above the 'godown' (warehouse) that abutted the Hogues' new house in Shibpur, across the Hugli River from the main part of British Kolkata. The young couple lived independently but joined the family for meals. Harriet was delighted to have a piano of her own. She took pride in showing off her new husband as they drove The Course in a curricle in the evenings, boasting that they could overtake everyone else.

The newly-married couple were soon separated by the pressure of business as Ritchie was charged with a major transport of goods for China and Sydney. In Sydney, Ritchie met his in-laws for the first time and the impression that he made on this visit may have sparked the caution in John Blaxland's stance to him. Meanwhile, Harriet gave birth to their daughter, Elizabeth (known as 'Eliza'), in Kolkata in August 1817 and fretted about her husband's absence.

Sati and cholera

Two of Harriet's oft-told tales concerned events witnessed during this time—sati and cholera—and both evoked an atmosphere of random death as a feature of life in India. Harriet provided an eye-witness account of the death of a native widow through sati (self-immolation) which would have riveted her listeners given the fascination that this religious practice held for the British. Her story-telling skills harnessed the semi-erotic power of the gothic romance: "Before bathing she took off every ornament giving to each a portion, then walking into the water. She came forth afterwards in a simple white muslin chudda, wet and dripping, clinging to her dusky form. Thus she returned a willing sacrifice. On mounting the pyre in an instance flames burst forth, amidst the wildest shouts, accompanied by tomtoms, brass trumpets, cymbals and gongs. Thick volumes of smoke shut out from view whatever may have passed in the last struggles."

Harriet claimed to have witnessed the last sati in Kolkata in 1817 but the practice of sati was not criminalised until Lord Bentinck's Regulation XVII in 1829. However, in 1817 there was a circular prepared which proposed increased proscription to the notions existing in law as to the conditions under which sati could and could not be considered legal (i.e., voluntary, age of widow, care of any children). The Governor General, the Earl of Moira, decided not to pursue it further due to concerns about continuing debates within Hindu religion as well as possibility of increasing its occurrence as act of protest against British regulation.[41]

Living so close to the river, Harriet witnessed the spread of death from the 1817 outbreak of cholera. "How to dispose of the dead became a serious question, without reference to caste nearly all were thrown into the river. Strong as the current always is, naked bodies were seen in every direction, with numbers of crows and vultures devouring the bodies as they sat.

The little dead infants became the prey of the adjutant birds standing in rows on the banks."

When her daughter's ayah fell ill, Harriet undertook to direct her care, much to the shock of her aunt who then insisted on Harriet being quarantined, semi-broiled in a hot bath and fumigated with frankincense.

Harriet described with ghoulish relish how superstition and blame spread and how a local witch's curse resulted in the subsequent deaths of a successive clergy: Bishops Middleton (who was rumoured to have been poisoned by finely-cut human hair put in his food, but who actually died of sunstroke 1822); Heber (who was found dead in his bath in 1826); and Cotton (who fell from a plank when disembarking from his budgerow—though not till 1866). Harriet could have also mentioned John Thomas James, who was Bishop from 1827-1828 and died at the age of forty-two while taking a sea voyage for his health, and John Matthias Turner, who was Bishop from 1829-1831 and who also died in office.[42,43] Things did improve briefly for Bishops in Kolkata, since Bishop Daniel Wilson, who became Bishop of Kolkata in 1832, lived to eighty and died there on 2nd January 1858.

Agra

When Ritchie returned, Uncle Hogue announced his decision to retire to England, and Ritchie was placed in charge of extending the company's reach northward. For Harriet, the loss of the support of her uncle was a personal blow but, from an economic perspective, it should have sounded an alarm bell. The Hogue's return to England was part of a growing tide of merchants who recognised that the glory days of the East India Company were over.⁴⁴ For those entrepreneurs with less experience, such as the Ritchies, the remaining opportunities were a lure they couldn't resist.

A flotilla was assembled for their journey up the river system to Agra. A large budgerow with two cabins accommodated Harriet and Ritchie, with their daughter Eliza and her ayah. Six smaller boats followed carrying their furniture, luggage and their twenty-five servants: including one kansuma (head servant); two kidmutgars (Muslim table servants); four bearers (principal servants involved in purchasing supplies); one cook; one assistant sweeper (cleaner); one keeper for cows and goats; one keeper for the dogs; one istri wala (laundry); as well as four sepoys (Indian soldiers in British service) to guard against dacoits (bandits). The tedium of the long hot journey through to the Yamuna River (formerly Jumna River) was broken by occasional stays at military stations to change the sepoys.

The worry about dacoits was not unjustified. Half-way to Agra, Harriet described: "...and so it happened about Buxar one dark night that two of these gentry swam off to the budgerow without clothes of any kind, head closely shaved and oiled from head to foot, making it impossible to hold them if caught; but timely alarm was given and a few shots fired when a grand splashing was heard in the water."

Social life in Agra was different from both Kolkata and Sydney. In Sydney, the Governor was a senior military officer and so senior military officers and associated civil servants enjoyed the highest status, followed by the landed free settlers, and then the merchants in the town, with former convicts ('expirees'/emancipists, ticket-of-leave) tailing above convicts serving their time and the native population. In Agra, Harriet found the prominent class to be civilians, then merchants, and then the military. As Harriet reported it, since their agency was "in the civil line", they were welcomed as members of the former group, which meant that the young couple were very much in demand socially. Their first son, Arthur, was born in Agra in August 1819, a couple of months after their arrival. They planned and built their new home on the banks of the river. From their veranda, Harriet looked across the river to the Taj Mahal. The mausoleum had been built in the 1600s by the Mughal emperor, Shah Jahan, for the tomb of his much-loved wife but its restoration would not begin until the early 1900s.

8 TAJ MAHAL IN EARLY 1800S

"*The Taje Mahal, Agra*" Aquatint, drawn and engraved in 1801 by Thomas and William Daniell (original held in British Library, public domain).

The view of the ruins should have been a warning. The Ritchies were engaging in a lavish social life when the business had yet to be established in that region. Ritchie faced the dilemma whether to stay on location to ensure growth or to travel to build trade links with China. The couple's relationship was placed under extreme stress.

When three-year-old Eliza was struck down by severe dysentery, Harriet panicked: "...nothing could be thought of than at once sending her to my mother."

Harriet fled with both Eliza and Arthur to Kolkata and shipped Eliza off to Sydney in the care of her ayah. Even for the time, the decision was unusual, particularly as Eliza was so unwell. Harriet's story of Eliza's journey suggested an attempt to convince her readers (and herself) that this decision was sensible: after all, the servant was trustworthy; the ship was owned by the company; when the ship had to put into Mauritius for repairs Eliza was looked after by Lady Farquhar, the Governor's wife; and, when Eliza arrived in Sydney, their great friend in Sydney, Captain Piper, took her up to Newington himself. However, Harriet had no choice. Within a week of Eliza's departure, she gave birth to her son, Alexander (known as "Alec") in May 1821. Harriet would have had no wish to repeat Mrs Murray's experience of labour at sea. As it was, with insufficient time to travel back to Agra, her confinement took place once more in the absence of her husband.

Putting her worries about Eliza's safety out of her mind, Harriet headed north again. She met up with Ritchie half-way, at Varanasi (formerly Benares) and they travelled together to Delhi, undertaking the last stage in a train of elephants, camels, horses, and bullock carts. The Ritchies might have been traveling in state, but this was nothing compared to luxurious lifestyle they would see during their visit with Sir David Ochterlony, the British Resident at Delhi. Ochterlony was a celebrated general with the East India Company and renown (or rather, infamous) for his embrace of the Mughal lifestyle, having lived in India for most of his life. Dalrymple, in his 2003 book on the 'White Mughals' told the apocryphal tale of how "every evening all thirteen of his consorts used to process around Delhi behind their husband, each on the back of her own elephant" and described Ochterlony's adoption of Indian dress (including turban).[45] Ochterlony was in his sixties when the Ritchies met him, and it was his secretary, Mr Frazer, who acted as their guide around the local historical sites before they returned to Agra.

It may have been on this long journey overland that Harriet "...had the courage to visit a tiger's lair with some friends, soon after the tigress left her cubs in search of food" (as described in family tales).[46] Courage was one way to describe it, but coming between a tigress and her cubs could be described in other ways.

The excitements of this journey may have shored up their marriage for a while but, back in Agra, financial pressure and illness returned and the relationship developed fractures. Harriet became gravely ill and resolved to return to Sydney with her sons. She was so unwell that she had to be carried on board the budgerow back to Kolkata. Richie did not accompany her. By the time they reached Kolkata, two-year-old Arthur had also fallen ill and so she had to "take lodgings" till he recovered sufficiently to travel further.

Once at sea on the *John Bull*, they recovered their health to the extent that on arriving at Hobart Town, Harriet was mainly concerned about buying a bonnet in preparation for their arrival in Sydney (since bonnets hadn't been the fashion during the eight years she had been in India).

5   The French Commodore

The reunion with her daughter and her family was joyous—Harriet was happy to be back at Newington. She was able to catch up with her brother George in Sydney for their sister's wedding. At seventeen, Anna was another very young bride when she married Thomas Walker in January 1823. The society wedding was a talking point as Anna wore a scarf which had been woven from raw silk she had produced. In order to promote the silk industry, Governor Brisbane had offered a small grant of land to the first in the colony to produce a pound of silk by a fixed date, and Anna had set about the task. Mulberry leaves were collected from the government gardens and distributed by the bushel. The family story was that Anna "was beaten by an old woman whose silk was very coarse"[47] but that Anna received a consolation gift of an amethyst cross and a gold chain. George, then twenty-one and working for Dent & Co, had taken Anna's raw silk to Guangzhou (formerly Canton) where it was made into her wedding scarf.

It didn't take long before the novelty of being back at home wore off: "I longed to return to my husband and home at Agra. My father, however, would not listen to the proposal, saying 'Ritchie must come for you'. Under this unjust restriction I was detained four years solely against my will."

The reason for his stand may have been protective. As a businessman, John would have kept a close eye on international trade and may well have been aware of the financial threats to the East India Company's agency houses. In addition, he may have developed a dim view of Ritchie and the nature of his business. Given the time period and the trade routes followed, the company's business may have involved the opium trade between India and China.⁴⁸ John Blaxland was a hard-headed and realistic entrepreneur in the sense of building capital, but unlikely to approve of the opium trade (and hence this disapproval might have formed not only part of his concerns in relation to Ritchie, but also contributed to the tension that existed between himself and his son George).

Either Ritchie's business was too compromised for him to afford to sail on one of the firm's ships to Sydney or the couple's relationship was hanging by a thread, as it was not until four years after Harriet's return, that Ritchie arrived on 6ᵗʰ August 1825 to collect her. Immediately upon his arrival, Ritchie set about making a series of acquisitions: a house and grounds between Pitt and Castlereagh Streets, opposite Betts Hotel; a government grant for 1,600 acres of land with assigned convict servants; and 100 head of cattle (with the agent, Robert Campbell).

For Harriet, Ritchie's purchases must have suggested that their finances were holding up better than she had expected, and her anger at his long delay in coming to get her would have escalated. In Harriet's memoirs she blamed her father, not Ritchie, for preventing her return to India. However, there was little doubt that she set about making Ritchie pay for his tardiness through her flirtation with the visiting French Commodore, Baron Hyacinthe de Bougainville.

Bougainville's father (Louis-Antoine de Bougainville) was the first Frenchman to circumnavigate the globe and Hyacinthe de Bougainville followed in his footsteps.⁴⁹ In 1825, he commanded a French naval expedition to Macau, Manila and New South Wales. It was the second occasion that he had been to Sydney, having participated in the Baudin expedition to Australia as a young midshipman in 1800–1802. On this second visit in 1825, he was in his mid-forties when he met twenty-five-year-old Harriet. Although she omitted all mention of him in her memoirs, he described their whirlwind romance during August–September in his personal notebooks.[50] A painting of Bougainville portrayed the ultimate Frenchman: a tall handsome man with curling dark hair and a dimple in his chin, leaning negligently against the rail of his ship.

9 BARON HYACINTHE DE BOUGAINVILLE

French painting from around 1830, and reproduced in Jean Randier's, *"La Royale: L'histoire illustree de la Marine nationale francaise"* 1972 (image from Wikimedia Commons, public domain).

"The Gentlemen of the Colony intend giving a Ball and Supper, on the 7th instant, to Commodore the Baron DE BOUGAINVILLE, and the Officers of the French ships of war, La Thetis and L'Esperance. This National compliment will be effected by subscription."

The Sydney Gazette and New South Wales Advertiser, Thursday 1 September, 1825, page 2.[51]

Their first meeting on Saturday 21st August 1825 took place at Newington where, after being shown around, Bougainville joined the family for dinner and an evening of music. He noted only that: "Three pretty young ladies were present: Miss Louisa, and her sisters. Mrs Ritchie is jolly and lively."

Bougainville returned the Blaxland's hospitality with lunch on board his corvette, *L'Espérance,* on Wednesday 7th September. Within days, Harriet and Bougainville were dancing together at a small ball hosted by Captain Piper on Saturday 10th September. Bougainville was captivated: "...I danced like a young beau (Mrs Ritchie is a beautiful woman with a jealous husband)."

They saw each other at Newington over the next two days and, on Monday 12th September, he wrote: "I found that I was more and more attracted to Mrs Ritchie, perhaps too much, and even now as I look back, how I miss her!" On Saturday 17th September, Bougainville visited the Balcombes: "...where Mrs Ritchie had pledged she would be; we enjoyed a romantic tête-à-tête and promised to meet the next day at midnight on board."

By the next morning, Harriet must have thought better of the planned assignation, since she wrote Bougainville a letter, saying that she "...had been obliged to go to Newington due to a prior engagement." Bougainville lamented: "Mrs R. haunts my thoughts, what a pity I became acquainted with her so late in the day! Beloved Harriet!"

The next evening, poor Bougainville had to suffer through a dinner party held by the Rossys, where: "...Mr and Mrs R. were seated next to each other to my deep chagrin."

If Harriet's design was to make Ritchie jealous, then she had succeeded. He took matters in hand, writing a challenge to Bougainville to meet him ashore in the Botanic Garden, Farm Cove. Like Harriet, Bougainville reconsidered his position: "...the prospect of being confronted with an angry husband, the angriest in the world, and above all the futility of such a course of action on the very eve of my departure induced me to combat the strong desire to see her one more time."

Finally, on Wednesday 24th September, Bougainville set sail, writing: "My heart is heavy and I wish now that we had sailed a month earlier...At 4.30 pm, we lost sight of the lighthouse from the topmast and, a little later, of the land from the deck. Everything then faded into the distance. I shall perhaps never again set eyes on these shores where on two separate occasions, at different stages of my life, I have experienced the joy of loving and of being loved! Farewell, happy days spent under the spell of mutual love! Alas, how fleeting you were! And how painful are the days that follow a parting that is bound to last forever!"

Bougainville never married, becoming Rear-Admiral of the French Navy in 1838 and dying in 1846. Bougainville's ardour was intense but Harriet's feelings were harder to know. That she started her flirtation in order to provoke Ritchie was evident, but if her plans for a midnight assignation had become more generally known, then she would have incurred far greater social consequences than a jealous husband. Harriet may have found herself swept up by her own unexpected return of Bougainville's passion but then, with time to reflect, found herself making what might have been the first mature decision of her life.

Ritchie acted quickly to remove Harriet from temptation and began preparations for their return to India. They made the decision to leave their children in the care of Reverend Frederick Wilkinson and his wife. The ostensible reason was "so as time should not be lost in their education." Educational opportunities in the colony had improved greatly in the period Harriet had been away, and Wilkinson was involved in trying to set up a grammar school in Parramatta.[52] However, Eliza was seven, Arthur was six, and Alec was five. The placement of the children under the care of others outside the family underscored the strained relationship with her parents that had developed over the past four years. The leaving of the children, coupled with Ritchie's acquisitions in Sydney, also raised the likelihood that, at least for Ritchie, there was full awareness of what awaited them back in Kolkata. In early January, they sailed from Sydney on the *Katherine Stewart Forbes*.

6   Destitution

10 MEETING THE PILOT BOAT AT SAND HEADS
"*At the Sand Heads: The Pilot Brig*" in the Bay of Bengal. Anonymous tinted stone lithograph published in about 1850 (public domain, http://ancestryimages.com).

While they were still in the Bay of Bengal, they received bad news: "On reaching the Sand Heads a fearful doom met us. The firm of Hogue Davidson Robertson and Ritchie, of sixty years standing, the wealthiest, had failed! …drawing with it the destruction of nearly half the other mercantile houses in Kolkata. As a partner and held responsible, though absent at the time, Ritchie on arrival in order to be safe from prosecution, could only reside beyond the Maratha Ditch (formerly Mahratta Ditch), where the English laws did not extend. A house was therefore taken for him till his Brother Masons of the Star-in-the-East Lodge could place him on board of a ship sailing for England, intending there to join his own family in Scotland."

The precipitating events behind this financial crash were many.[53,54] From 1820, there was a severe depression in British India. The East India Company had lost most of its trade monopoly (through the Charter Act of 1813) except opium, salt and tea. Also, the Burma war in 1824 had interrupted shipping.[55,56] As partners in agency houses (such as the Hogues) withdrew their investment and returned to England, some agencies fell due to lack of capital, and their interdependence led to a snowball effect.

Ritchie sailed on the *William Young* but Harriet did not flee with him, finding herself "...utterly cast upon the world without money." However, this was destitution, Harriet-style.

She was taken in by Mr and Mrs Allport, who happened by coincidence to be living in the same house where Harriet and Ritchie had made their first home with the Hogues in Shibpur, Kolkata. Harriet also described the great kindness and financial support of Babu Russomay Dutt, who had worked for her uncle for many years. Since the financial crisis had drastically reduced shipping movements, Harriet had to wait in Kolkata for five months to obtain passage on a ship to back New South Wales. She left her servant, Sarah Mott, behind in Kolkata, despite Sarah having accompanied her from Sydney. Harriet described Sarah as having been a "special comfort" and a "friend" during this time of difficulty but, with Sarah's interests in mind, Harriet obtained a position with a respectable family who were going back to England. Sarah must have had her own ideas as to what was in her interests since, Harriet reported, "I was told that on her way to her new mistress in Chowringee (now Chourangi), the poor girl was run away with by a gentleman of my acquaintance."

As Harriet finally set sail aboard the *Marquis of Lansdowne*, she described her suffering: "The prospects of a fifth voyage...in a small ship compared to the last, friendless and alone with only a native ayah as attendant, crushed me altogether. The voyage was a perfect blank in everything to me."

The journey wasn't so much a blank as to prevent her from writing a riveting account of a suicidal fire-worshipping head steward. The head steward practised Zoroastrianism—a religion from what is now Iran in which the good spirit of Ahura Mazdah is represented by fire (but also by water and earth) in contrast with evil (dead matter).[57] The head steward kept a candle burning by the ship's mast and refused to obey orders to extinguish it. The punishment was flogging but the man leapt overboard rather than suffer the shame. Harriet ended her tale with the man swimming away from the ship: "Each time the boat neared him he dived under and eluded the grasp of the sailors till, quite exhausted, the poor man threw up his arms and with a wild shriek sunk for ever. The last rays of the setting sun give light in the horizon to this awful and grand picture."

On this voyage, the route was via Jakarta (formerly Batavia), and Harriet accompanied friends to visit a gentleman she described as the "Rothschild of the island" whose wealth had come from the sale of birds' nests to China. Listening to "sweet Italian music" played by his band of sixty musicians, Harriet watched with awe as "...there came twelve young girls dressed in the finest white Dacca muslin, confined by zones of pure gold round their waists, bracelets of jewels and splendid earrings—

each carrying a silver tray covered with scarlet velvet on which was coffee in outer cups of gold filigree, with Sevre china. The next girl followed with liqueurs in exquisite bottles and glasses, then came sweet-meats on another with fruits, preserves, cakes etc., each girl presenting a different offering." Harriet was given many expensive presents, including a small piano and numerous "live curiosities" of local fauna and flora. Unfortunately, her bad luck continued, as most of these were lost in a storm at sea.

"Jan. 8. Arrived the ship Marquis of Lansdown[e], R. Noyes, 208 tons, from Calcutta, Singapore, and last from Batavia, 12th November, with 10 tubs sugar candy, 128 bags and 55 casks of sugar, 27 pipes Lisbon wine, 5 ditto Teneriffe, 9 half ditto ditto, 5 cases shot, 50 boxes hyson skia tea, 10 ditto black, 1 ditto hyson green, 1 ditto imperial, 3 packages of hyson, 1 ditto gunpowder, 1 ditto black, 300 bags rice, 4 boxes of bandannas, 29 ditto tea, 50 ditto dry ginger, 30 ditto saltpetre, 2 pipes Maderia, 151 kegs tobacco, 1 ditto cloves 2 ditto nutmegs, 1 bale Patna palam pores, 40 bundles twine, 15 boxes cheroots, 1 bale canvas bags, 8 boxes curry powder, 1 ditto cayenne pepper, 1 box Dacca muslins, 563 half chests black tea, 25 cannisters sugar, one trunk wearing apparel, several packages for G. Cartwright, Raine &, Co., T. G. Pitman and Jones & Co. among which are 139 baskets sugar, 61 bags pepper, 15 packages canvas, 30 kegs crackers, 6 cases cordial, 6 bags wax, and 10 tierces vinegar. Passengers - Mr. J. and Mrs. Lord and 3 children, Mrs. Ritchie, Mr. J. F. Goodair and 2 women servants. With six prisoners, namely - 4 transported soldiers, and 2 runaways from Sydney. Agent - Mr. Bethune."

Tasmanian news from the Hobart Town Gazette in The Sydney Gazette and New South Wales Advertiser, Thursday 25 January, 1827, page 3.[58]

7   Doctor Ritchie

By February, 1827, Harriet was back with her family on the Newington estate near Parramatta but it was not for another six months that she found out that Ritchie had died within weeks of leaving Kolkata on the *William Young*. Society gossip was that Ritchie "died of drinking after separating from her" (as Lady Gipps relayed to Lady Franklin years later).[59]

11 First Agricultural Fair in Parramatta, 1823

This image is from Parramatta Heritage Centre Research Library photo collection LSP00854 (published with permission).

The previous four years at Newington while waiting for Ritchie had been difficult enough but, now widowed, she found herself dependent on her father for support. The Pitt Street property which Ritchie had bought during his brief stay in the colony had to be sold to settle Ritchie's bankruptcy debts but, through the offices of the agent Mr Campbell, she retained her interest in the land and the cattle.

Harriet recalled this time in her life with acrimony: "The experiment of families living together after long years of separation in the world, should never be made, especially before character has had time to develop. In my case, during the latter part of this grievous trial no persecution was considered too bitter, requiring on my part every effort of endurance for my children's sake in our then penniless and powerless condition."

Her father and mother would have also felt the strain since their farmhouse was too small for the large extended family. The building for the grand Newington House did not commence until 1829 and was not finished until 1832. Harriet's siblings who were closest in age had left: her brother John was looking after the Fordwich property in the Hunter,[60] George was still at sea, and Anna Walker was living at Rhodes on the southern bank of the Parramatta River (before moving to Tasmania in 1832). However, the household was filled with her younger brothers and sisters as well as herself and her children. There were six adults (her parents, herself, and her sisters—Jane Elizabeth Blaxland, Louisa Australia Blaxland, Eliza Maria Blaxland) and six children (her siblings—Edward James Blaxland, Mary Ellen Blaxland, Arthur Blaxland; and her three young children—Eliza Ritchie, Arthur Ritchie, Alec Ritchie). Even after the building of the new house was completed in 1832, they would have been very short of space.

12 NEWINGTON HOUSE, PARRAMATTA

Photograph from around 1930 when the house was part of Newington College. Image from *Newington College Archives* (public domain).

The census of 1828 noted that the estate housed seventy-two adults (of whom twelve were female) apart from the Blaxlands themselves. Of the twelve females, eight were convicts and the others were former convicts. Of the former convicts, one was the cook, forty-five-year-old Mary Holder, and the other three were married to workers on the estate: Sarah Champion, wife of the blacksmith (with seven children under eleven years); Mary Knowles, wife of the shoemaker (no children); and Mrs Lamb, wife of the gardener. Of the eight convicts, three were married to other convicts and the other five worked in the house: Susan Barnett, housemaid; Jane Blake and Eliza Picket, needle-women; Mary Fause and Sarah McDonald, laundresses.[61]

Newington was full to bursting and Harriet struggled to find a role for herself: "The only consolation left me under these circumstances was watching over the education of my three children and otherwise occupying myself among the people of the Estate as Sister of Mercy, obtaining at last the title of 'Doctor Ritchie'."

13 JOHN BLAXLAND IN 1832

"*John Blaxland, Esq.*" Watercolour painted by R. Read in 1832. Image from the collections of the State Library of NSW, Catalogue ML 308 (freely available to publish without permission).

As difficult as successive governors of the colony found her father to deal with, he had achieved a social prominence that could not be ignored. When Governor Darling expanded the size and role of the Legislative Council in 1829,[62] he appointed John to one of the new seats. John Blaxland's background and life experience promoted his sense of the rights of the individual made him a strong supporter of the right to Trial by Jury for the colony (which was not introduced until 1847).

"On Tuesday evening, as Mr John Blaxland was returning home from the races, in his carriage, when he had got about half way down the avenue leading from the public road to his house, he was encountered by four men, two of them armed with muskets and the other two with pistols. Having secured the coachman, they took the carriage aside into the bush, and demanded of Mr Blaxland an instant surrender of his cash; he told them he had none about him; they replied that he had better be cautious what he said, for that they were determined to search him from head to foot, and if they found a simple sixpence more than he acknowledged, they would blow his brains out on the spot. Having repeated his assertion that he had only a shilling or two in his pockets, they ordered him to strip to the skin; he said that having very infirm health, such an act of violence might cost him his life; and while they were considering what should be done, the Miss Blaxlands rode up from the house to meet their father; the robbers pointed their pieces at them, and ordered them to come on pain of being shot; but much to the honour of their courage, the young ladies immediately turned their horses' heads, and galloped back to the house; on which the bushrangers, fearing a strong force would be sent in pursuit of them, took to their heels."

The Sydney Gazette and New South Wales Advertiser, Thursday 22 April, 1830, page 2.[63]

Something of John Blaxland's stubbornness shows in the story of his encounter with bushrangers in 1830 as reported in the local newspaper when he resisted giving robbers any money by claiming to have none.[64] He presented himself to the robbers as "infirm" although, at sixty-two years, he was very much in his prime with another fifteen years of life ahead. His prevarication about the amount of money he had on him no doubt reflected his reputation as keeping his own (and the government's) purse strings tight rather than his being skint after his day at the races. The paper described how the two "Miss Blaxlands" scared the brigands away. They were most likely to have been Jane and Louisa who were in their twenties when the robbery occurred. Their response to the armed robbery suggested that Harriet wasn't the only member of the family prepared to take a risk.

The Dowling proposal

About a year after Harriet had returned to Sydney, Justice James Dowling arrived to take up his position as a puisne judge in the Supreme Court of New South Wales in 1828. Dowling brought his wife and six children aged between four and twelve years old. Mrs Dowling (formerly Maria Sheen) had been a friend of Harriet's mother in their school days, and so the two families quickly became closely acquainted. Harriet's brother George, who was then based in Sydney after leaving Dent & Co, later married Dowling's daughter, Maria Dowling. While the wives were close, their husbands would not prove to be companionable. Dowling's Irish origins and lack of family background were not in his favour. Additionally, Dowling's quick wit and level of education may have been disconcerting for the more ponderous John Blaxland.

Harriet felt that her unhappy situation as a dependent widow at Newington aroused the sympathy of Mrs Dowling. Mrs Dowling, who had been unwell for some time, died in August 1834 and, as reported by Harriet, Mrs Dowling's concern for her young family meant that, during her illness, she had pleaded with her husband that he should marry again following her death. Of course, in Harriet's version of events, her pleading specified that his choice should fall upon her. However, after his wife's death Dowling first turned to Jane Blaxland to provide a mother for his children (as he later described in a letter to his son James Sheen Dowling).[65]

Twenty-eight-year-old Jane refused his proposal. Why Jane refused was unclear. After all, Dowling was a loving father, intelligent companion and a man of high status in the community. Possibly, her father would have disapproved of the match, not only because of his opinion of Dowling but also because of George being married to Maria Dowling, i.e., Jane would become her brother's 'mother'. However, another possibility for Jane's refusal related to the timing of Dowling's proposal. Jane had just met Baron Charles von Hügel, a strikingly handsome gentleman and a distinguished naturalist.

The Baron, nudging forty when he visited New South Wales, had been betrothed to an Hungarian countess (Melanie Zichy-Ferraris), but his hopes had been dashed when she married the Austrian chancellor, Klemens Wenzel, Prince von Metternich. Licking his wounds, he embarked on an extensive grand tour from 1831 to 1836, taking in Kashmir and the Punjab, New Zealand and Australia. By the time he met the Blaxlands he had already met the woman he would eventually marry, Elizabeth Farquharson, the daughter of a Scottish military officer he met in India in 1833 but to whom he wasn't betrothed until 1847. However, neither his broken heart nor his future prospects distracted him from his botanical pursuits nor dimmed his eye for attractive women and he described both pursuits in detail in his extensive journals.[66]

He met Jane Blaxland at Newington not long after the unexpected death from consumption of her sister Eliza Maria (married to Major Henry William Breton). Although the household was grief-stricken and in subdued mourning, he was impressed by both Jane and Louisa: "…(their) minds take an interest in everything that appeals to them, and whose degree of cultivation and talent in this remote continent greatly astonished me."

During his visit Harriet was unwell and rarely to be seen. When he did meet her he was surprised by how young she looked, saying she could be mistaken for a "slightly older sister of her daughter" even though Harriet was then thirty-three and Eliza Ritchie was seventeen.

However, it was Jane who captured his attention: "…I soon settled on Miss Jane Blaxland as my favourite, whose beautiful dark eyes, exquisitely shaped, expressed an unsurpassable goodness of heart. I have never seen more expressively arched eyebrows, their almost unnaturally dark line marking the outline of her intelligent forehead, framed by luxuriant blonde curls. In fact, I know of no one with finer features or a more pleasant expression, set off by a noble, slender figure. All these advantages are combined with an absence of pretension which is the mark of a steady, even character. A superficial observer will take this for coldness and in this he will be mistaken, although no trace of passion, of whatever kind, will ever be revealed to him."

14 Baron Charles von Hügel

Painting by Joseph Neugebauer in 1851 and printed in the biography, "*Charles von Hügel, April 25, 1795–June 2, 1870*" by his son Anatole von Hügel in 1903 (public domain).

Few men of Jane's acquaintance would have been as able as the visiting naturalist to contribute to her botanical knowledge. The Baron was flattered enough by her attention to record her comment that his knowledge served to "...elevate the minds of those who listen to you, to give those who live out their lives in quiet solitude a wider view of the world and of creation."

Perhaps, in refusing Dowling, Jane dreamed of a future with the Baron. She continued to correspond with von Hügel and to send him botanical specimens of interest even up to six years later. However, the Baron, writing from Vienna to Jane in 1840, thanked her for sending some seeds but, at the same time, seemed to be trying to politely extinguish any hopes she might have still harboured. He wrote: "To see once more Australia is still the dearest hope of my heart, but I am afraid that one thing is wanting to enjoy my return visit: youth."[67]

15 JANE BLAXLAND IN AROUND 1835

"*Jane Elizabeth Blaxland*" oil painting. Image from the collections of the State Library of NSW, Catalogue ML 446 (freely available to publish without permission).

For whatever reason, Jane made her decision and Dowling went on to propose to Harriet. It would be hard to imagine, in the close proximity of those at Newington House, that Harriet did not know of the earlier proposal and its rejection, despite her discretion on the matter in her memoir. Harriet's love of a good tale meant that a more romantic version was preferred.

In a moment of spectacular insensitivity, Harriet recorded that, with the death of Maria, George's wife and Dowling's daughter: "...this melancholy bereavement the last objection was removed for Judge Dowling marrying me."

Thirty-five-year-old Harriet and fifty-two-year-old Dowling were married at St John's Church in Parramatta by Reverend Samuel Marsden on the 1st September, 1835.

16 ST JOHN'S CHURCH, PARRAMATTA

"*St John's Church, Parramatta*" by unknown artist in around 1820. Image from the collections of the State Library of NSW, Catalogue SV1B/Parr/2 (freely available to publish without permission).

8   The Second Lady in the Colony

Over two months later, news of their marriage had not reached her sister Anna Walker in Tasmania,[68] so it appeared that Jane, usually a keen correspondent, wasn't wholly pleased by the turn of events. Predictably, nor was John Blaxland supportive of the marriage, refusing to pay the £50 which Harriet sought for her trousseau. However, this was a not inconsiderable sum: roughly $AUD 7,000 today. Instead, Harriet prevailed upon her cousin Eliza's husband, Dr Thomas Forster, for the amount. As he was an army surgeon, this support was generous indeed.

Everything about Dowling and Harriet suggested they were pragmatists, and theirs was a marriage that suited them both well, as it provided care and support for each other and for their respective children. Beyond these practical reasons for marriage, Harriet described her feelings toward Dowling with strong emotion: "Bound by such nobility of heart and nature for ever, what woman could feel it in her power to do enough for such a husband, and truly no two beings were happier than we for nearly ten years, with our two sets of nearly grown up children."

Harriet's new home was at Brougham Lodge (close to the current junction of Kings Cross, Darlinghurst). Dowling had named his residence after the English Whig politician and statesman, Henry Brougham, who had recommended him for the post in the Supreme Court.[69] Their combined household was as numerous as that at Newington. The Ritchie children were Eliza Ritchie (nineteen), Arthur Ritchie (sixteen) and Alec Ritchie (fourteen). Of the Dowling children, five were living at the time of their marriage—Vincent Francis Woodcock Dowling (nineteen), Anne Dowling (seventeen—sadly, dying the following year), James Sheen Dowling (sixteen), Eliza Dowling (fourteen), and Susannah Dowling (twelve). This environment of so many energetic and intelligent young people was an ideal milieu for Harriet. Her step-son, James Sheen Dowling, recorded: "...her conversational powers were great; her mind was stored with knowledge, and she could talk by the hour about the early days of the colony, which to me was most interesting."[70] (See the Appendices for a full list of the Ritchie and Harriet's Dowling step-children at the time of their marriage.)

BROUGHAM LODGE IN 1848, THE RESIDENCE OF THE DOWLING FAMILY.
Brougham Terrace in Victoria Street, Darlinghurst, now stands on this Site.

17 BROUGHAM LODGE, DARLINGHURST IN 1848

Residence of the Dowling Family. Image from the collections of the State Library of NSW, Catalogue SPF 3529 (freely available to publish without permission).

Dowling had supported himself through his legal studies by writing law reports for the London papers and one of his important legacies to the legal system in New South Wales was his 500 reports of many significant legal cases that he oversaw in the Supreme Court.[71] Harriet described him as: "... a witty Irish gentleman, a variety now but seldom seen, but on the bench he was the stern English Judge." His son, James Sheen Dowling, described him similarly as having: "...all the attributes of an Irishman, he was full of fun, of a very happy disposition, fond of his joke, and in his rambles would converse with almost everybody he met."[72]

Such strolls were most often on foot, as he hated to ride, often ending up leading the horse. One day, he rambled into trouble. He and Harriet had been staying over at Newington and for some reason he decided to rise early and head back into town (maybe he'd had enough of his father-in-law), only to be pulled up by an over-zealous constable as a suspected "convict-at-large" and taken to the watch-house before eventually convincing them of his identity.[73]

When Chief Justice Forbes was granted leave to return to England due to ill-health, he recommended Dowling to Governor Bourke for the position as Chief Justice. Justice Burton also sought the position but it was Dowling who was promoted and after his appointment as Chief Justice in 1837, he was knighted the following year. Dowling commented drily on this elevation saying: "The nickname has made many people wondrous civil to me."[74] As might be expected, Harriet's glee was unbounded: "To me, how great the change. Suddenly to find myself the second Lady in the colony."

The 'first Lady' in the colony was the governor's wife. By 1838, the Governor of New South Wales was Sir George Gipps who arrived that February with his wife and son. Harriet's social rounds included others with the title 'Lady' in the colony, such as Lady Forbes (who had returned with her retired husband, Sir

Francis Forbes). When Lady Franklin (the wife of Sir John Franklin, the famous Arctic explorer and Lieutenant-Governor, based in Tasmania) visited Sydney in 1839, she noted in her diary of Monday 15ᵗʰ July: "Visit from Lady Dowling—I observed to Lady Gipps that I thought her rather clever and pleasant—Lady Gipps agreed but not so Sir James whom she believed to be of low origin and who shewed it. She said the Chief Justice came next to Governor by reference to home. She had remarked that Lady Dowling and Lady O'Connell never came together—Lady O'Connell staid away when Lady Dowling was expected."[75]

This entry by Lady Franklin in her diary captured the sticky web of social relationships in the small community. Lady O'Connell was the daughter of Governor Bligh, arriving with him in 1806 as the wife of Lieutenant Putland, who died in 1808. In 1810, she married Maurice O'Connell.[76] The stand-off between the two women went back to the mutual hostility between their fathers which culminated in John's support of what became known as the 'rum rebellion' and Bligh's instigation of John's arrest and imprisonment at Cape Town.

Harriet would have enjoyed Lady Franklin's company immensely. Lady Franklin was an audacious traveller. She was the first white woman to make the journey to Sydney by coming overland from Melbourne and she did so without her husband (though with such an extensive retinue, that there were reputed to be rhymes about her as the Queen of Sheba in the market place).[77]

A Gentleman's Daughter

18 SIR JAMES DOWLING IN 1840

"*Sir James Dowling*" painted by J. Dennis. Image from the collections of the State Library of NSW, Catalogue ML 249 (freely available to publish without permission).

Harriet's responsibilities for her extended family lessened as the children grew up and moved away. James Sheen Dowling and Arthur Ritchie both headed to London to undertake legal studies in 1836. Dowling took Harriet's son, Alec Ritchie, under his wing and appointed him as his associate. When her daughter, Eliza Ritchie, married Charles Boydell in 1837, Harriet spared no effort for the wedding, compensating for her own two quiet weddings.

A Gentleman's Daughter

"Newington, 22nd May, 1837

My dear Anna,

When I closed my last letter to you, I thought to have written again immediately, but in these busy times a month passes like a few days & I am astonished to think I have not yet fulfilled my promise of giving an account of the wedding, which did not take place 'till the 2nd of this month—it certainly was the gayest I ever attended and we kept it up for two days in the good old style according to Mr Dowling's wish—We behaved most admirably on the occasion from the beginning to the end of the <u>two days</u>! And Harriotte bore the fatigue and anxiety of the whole affair with astonishing spirit and fortitude—the Breakfast she provided was handsome and well served—the Dinner good, and the Evening party very pleasant, now this, added to marrying a Daughter, was really much business for one day. The number at breakfast was 26—nearly the same party assembled at dinner—in the Evening we had many additions in the way of merry dancing Girls and Boys—Mr D was so elated that he proposed the party should assemble the following evening, which was gladly seconded by all—so after a picnic in Bondi Bay…we all met and danced the second evening most merrily away…I think I was never more fatigued."

Transcript of excerpts from Jane Blaxland's letter to her sister, Anna Walker, from the collections of the State Library of NSW, Catalogue Ab.50 (freely available to publish without permission).[78]

By 1842, Susannah Dowling had married the Reverend Charles Spencer, Eliza Dowling had married Arthur Hodgson, and Vincent Dowling was running the family estate on the Williams River, tributary of the Hunter River, near Dungog, New South Wales.

Harriet's relationship with her Blaxland family deteriorated further when the long-standing dispute with the Hogues about monies owed flared up again.[79] The £1,000 owed by John Blaxland to Uncle Hogue remained outstanding from 1828. After Uncle Hogue's death, his son, Arthur, travelled to Sydney in 1838[80] to press his claim for repayment. By that time, the debt was equivalent to nearly $AUD 2 million. John Blaxland refused to pay on the grounds that he considered this money was owed to his wife from her mother's estate. Due to the dispute, John directed Arthur Hogue to stay with the Dowlings rather than at Newington.

During Arthur Hogue's stay, Dowling took it upon himself to advise John that the dispute over the maternal estate was not relevant to the issue of the debt. Blaxland accused him of acting dishonourably by pushing the claim of the nephew and Dowling, understandably, took great offence. In a letter he wrote in 1841 to his son describing the events, he went so far as to describe John Blaxland in strongly negative terms: "...what with his own perverse ignorance, obstinacy and sordid love of money he has forfeited all claim to my respect."[81]

From 1838 until her father's final illness in 1845, Harriet was estranged from her parents, maintaining contact with George alone of her brothers and sisters. During this time, her brother John Marquet Blaxland died in May 1840. It would have been from the newspapers that she learned of the shipwreck of the

Clonmel steam ship in 1841 and the fortunate survival of all passengers, including her sister, Anna Elizabeth Walker.[82] In that period also, her sister Jane made her first trip to England but died there in March 1843. The same year, her sister Mary Ellen Molle died at the age of twenty-eight.

The estrangement meant that Harriet was very much on her own as Dowling became increasingly ill under the strain of his workload as Chief Justice of the Supreme Court. Dowling's workload had increased significantly when Justice Burton, still smarting at being refused the appointment as Chief Justice, decamped to the Supreme Court in Madras (Chennai) in 1844 where he was knighted. Harriet watched as Dowling's health deteriorated and she was outraged as Governor Gipps refused to grant him leave of absence to recover, despite numerous requests. She reported the Governor's reasons as: "The colony was so soon to undergo the change from bondage, as a penal colony to the Free Institutions of England, no other person was so duly qualified to conduct the business, and Sir James Dowling could not be spared."[83] The Order-in-Council directing the end of transportation of convicts to New South Wales had been given in 1840, but transportation continued to be a live issue even as late as 1849, when a 5,000 strong protest meeting was held at Circular Quay in Sydney to prevent the docking of the *Hashemy*, the last convict transport ship to New South Wales.[84]

Harriet described the final days before Dowling died on 27th September, 1844 with anguish: "When his life was actually despaired of Sir George Gipps relaxed his severity and said Sir James might seek change to England. A passage was immediately secured, cabins fitted with hot pipes and lined throughout with green baize, servant engaged, the Governor's state barge ordered and the day fixed for embarking. All too late! On that day the inestimable man expired."

Newspaper reports were suggestive of pneumonia as the cause of death.[85] Another report in the Sydney Morning Herald stated that he was: "...the victim of conscientious devotedness, throughout the long period of nearly seventeen years, to the interests of the public."[86] At his funeral, there were one hundred and five carriages in the procession which extended the six blocks from St James Church down to Campbell Street. Governor Gipps attended and the pall bearers were the most prominent gentlemen in the colony. At the burial at the family vault in Waverley Cemetery, the service was read by the Bishop of Australia, William Broughton. The bells of both St James Church and the Roman Catholic cathedral, St Mary's, tolled throughout the morning.[87]

Sir William Burton,[88] perhaps with a sense of guilt for leaving the crippling workload to Dowling, offered Harriet's son, Alec a clerical post with him in the courts of Madras (Chennai), which he accepted.

9   Forgiveness

Within a year of her husband's death, Harriet faced the death of her father at the age of seventy-seven: "In 1845, after an illness of three months, my father sent for me to nurse him, which I did, with others, night and day. At the last moment he pressed my hand and passed away on 5th August 1845."

Harriet's mother (sixty-eight years) and her sister Louisa (thirty-eight years) had the assistance of staff but their numbers were much reduced in comparison with Newington's hey-day. The house itself was run with the help of a butler, cook, housemaid, lady's maid, laundress, as well as a seamstress. Other staff included a coachman, gardener, and a yardman. Harriet viewed the call by her father as a plea for reconciliation and was grateful to be by his side at the end.

John Blaxland's involvement in pastoral, business and government affairs had long made him a respected member of the community.[89] A summary of John Blaxland's life in the newspaper stated: "By his family and friends he was universally beloved and by the public he was highly respected and admired for his uniform good sense, consistency, and the firmness which marked his political career."[90]

The goodwill, which Harriet felt following his death, rapidly dissipated when the contents of his will were made known. With her characteristic perspective on financial matters she noted: "On the will being opened my Brother George to his horror and amazement, found himself on the 12th August, disinherited without any reason given."

However, in the copy of John Blaxland's will available in the State Library of New South Wales (amongst the Walker family papers),[91] George Blaxland was left the same provision as was made for Harriet and her surviving sisters (Anna Elizabeth Walker, Louisa Australia Blaxland): namely, £2,000 to be paid within ten years with an annual payment of £200 with interest. This bequest would have provided Harriet with the equivalent a total of $AUD 408,000, or an annuity of $AUD 40,800 per year for ten years in terms of affordability of an average person's lifestyle for the time. In relation to George, the sole difference was that any outstanding debts that he owed to his father were to be deducted from his legacy. Presumably, George's debt had not been repaid before his father's death

Harriet's younger brothers—thirty-two-year-old Edward and twenty-nine-year-old Arthur—were the executors of the estate. Edward and Arthur were an integral part of the family's estates and associated enterprises, with Arthur having established his family at Fordwich, Broke in the Wollombi Valley.[92] At £100,000, John Blaxland's estate was substantial (current equivalence of over $AUD 200 million). However, Edward and Arthur faced the problem that their father had mortgaged the property in 1843. Maintaining the estate and the house for their mother and Louisa was going to be a challenge, with the total staffing level of nine domestic staff costing about £390 per annum[93] (currently equivalent in wage costs to over $AUD 800,000), not to mention the provisions (described above) for Harriet, Anna and Louisa which involved payments to be made over the next decade.

Edward and Arthur Blaxland dug in their heels when Harriet attempted to negotiate for her own legacy to be advanced so that she could assist her son Arthur Ritchie to finance his legal studies. It could have been that they had absorbed their father's concerns about Harriet's expenditure. However, it was as likely that the problem lay with the difficulties they were having in realising the value of the Newington Estate as the colony was still recovering from a dramatic rise in wages following the cessation of assigned convict labour and an economic recession affecting the value of land and stock during the early 1840s.

As well as the legacy from her father, as the widow of Sir James Dowling, Harriet had £200 voted to her annually by the Legislative Council of New South Wales. In terms of her ability to meet cost of living expenses, Harriet did not consider her income (totalling £400 or $AUD 81,600 in current terms) sufficient for her needs. In 1844, within days of Dowling's death, Harriet had petitioned Lord Stanley (Secretary of State for War and the Colonies) for a pension of £3,000 to be paid from the government pension fund (current equivalence about $AUD 600,000 per annum). Harriet would have been aware of a similar petition made a few months before by Lady Forbes, now also widowed.

Lord Stanley considered both petitions and, in true bureaucratic buck-passing style, replied to Governor Gipps as follows: "... the Government consider that it would be inexpedient to make any allowance...At the same time you are authorized to bring the claims of these ladies under the consideration of the Legislative Council, and with reference to the strong recommendations which you have in both cases received from almost every individual member of that body, you will intimate to the Council that you are prepared to assent to provision being made by annual vote, or otherwise, from funds at their disposal, for the relief of the applicants."[94]

Governor Gipps must have rued his strong support when his words were invoked in relation to his own budget. However, Harriet didn't take Lord Stanley's decision lying down. In 1847, she sailed for London to put her petition in person.

10   Home is a First-Class Cabin

Sea travel (first-class, of course) brought Harriet everything she enjoyed: company, conversation, a captive audience, cards and cabin service. Her wit and vivacity enlivened the trip for others, too. On her 1847 voyage, one of her fellow passengers was twenty-eight-year-old James Milbourne Marsh—a nephew of Lady Forbes and a friend of her elder son, Arthur Ritchie. Marsh was a keen diarist and through his journal entries,[95] Harriet sparkled as the inimitable Lady Dowling. He described her as a keen card player—chiefly whist and loo—as well as happy to participate in the passengers' amateur theatricals and to amuse the party with tales of India and Sydney scandal. He wrote on Thursday 1st April, "A fine day again, all the ladies on deck...The Captain today sang out 'Iceberg ahead' in order to make April Fools of the party. Lady Dowling jumped from one side of the ship to the other and on to the forecastle as nimbly as a deer."

As a passenger, she was high maintenance for the cabin crew. On Tuesday 20th April, "Lady Dowling did not make her appearance till after dinner. Some said she had taken disgust with the Captain for having stopped her glass of milk which she was in the habit of taking before breakfast." On Friday 30th April, he wrote, "Lady Dowling was in a great anger with the head steward. Her lamp went out, and she requested him to fill it again but he made answer that the lamp was too warm. Her Ladyship immediately jumped up in anger and took it off himself and attempted to light it herself."

The sailors on the voyage also suffered. When the ship passed through a mass of blue-bottles (Portuguese man o'war) on Thursday 13th May, specimens were brought on board in a bucket to interest the passengers. Harriet instructed the sailors to leave the bucket on deck so that she could sketch them later. As might have been foreseen, the bucket tipped over, and many of the barefooted sailors were stung and needed the attention of the ship's doctor.

On Sunday 30th May, about two weeks before their arrival in England, Marsh described how she capped off the voyage: "Last night Lady Dowling gave some wine very indiscreetly to the sailors, several of them got drunk, and the man at the wheel was discovered steering in an exactly opposite direction." Even for Harriet, this gregariousness appeared to be too much. Marsh added succinctly, "Lady Dowling did not make an appearance at all today."

Unlike many an acquaintance forged during a lengthy journey, Harriet's friendship with Marsh continued post disembarkation and for the rest of her life. While in England, she met up with Marsh and his fiancée, Miss Grace Pinnock, for sightseeing at the Tower of London and she was a guest at their wedding.

As much as she was enjoying herself, her mission was to press her claim for an increased pension, arguing for parity of her pension with the widows of Governors of the colony. By then, Lord Grey was the man responsible for the matter, but she had no more luck with him than Lord Stanley.[96]

Initially, Harriet stayed with her brother-in-law, Vincent Dowling, Editor of the prominent magazine, *Bell's Life in London*, in Norfolk Street, The Strand. During her stay there, as she excitedly informed Marsh, she met Charles Dickens and his wife. She set up house in Hampton Place, Regents Square with her son Arthur Ritchie who had completed his studies (BA, Barrister-at-Law). Her outlay for this establishment involved expenditure on furnishings and a twelve-month lease. Unfortunately for her hip-pocket, within three months Arthur would leave to join his brother, Alec, by accepting a position with what was then the Supreme Court in Madras (Chennai)—later, the High Court. Shortly after he arrived in India, Arthur married Mary Jane Hobbs, youngest daughter of the late Lieutenant-Colonel Hobbs of the Royal Engineers, on 4th November 1848,[97] and they went on to have one daughter, Helen (born 1851). Later, Alec married Frances Francklyn, daughter of the late Major Francklyn in 1854[98] and eventually became Chief Clerk of the Supreme Court in Madras (Chennai).

Her sons' location in India prompted her to incorporate lengthy stays there as part of her subsequent travels between England and Australia. Her first such visit began in August 1849 when she left London headed for Madras (Chennai) on the *Trafalgar*.[99] After a stay of about a year in India she arrived back in Sydney in April 1851 on the *Vimeira*.[100]

Her return to the colony may have been prompted by her mother's ill-health. Family reports suggested Harriet de Marquet Blaxland suffered a stroke after her husband's death in 1845, but lived on for some years. In January of 1852, at the age of seventy-four, Mrs Blaxland died at George's home in Fort Street, Sydney.[101]

Mrs Blaxland had managed to bear and raise ten children to adulthood, to run a household staffed by convict women, and to impress visiting dignitaries with her keen intelligence and wit. To the other older Blaxland sisters—Anna, Jane and Louisa — their mother was always "Dearest Mama" and her guidance had shaped their own extensive botanical knowledge and skilful drawing as well as that of her granddaughter, Anna Frances Walker, a painter of some note.[102] She had a strong character: "petticoat government" was the way Dowling described his mother-in-law's influence on John Blaxland's decision-making in a letter to his son.[103]

19 HARRIET DE MARQUET BLAXLAND

"*Harriott Blaxland*" oil painting thought to be painted by Maurice Felton in around 1835. From the collections of the State Library of NSW, Catalogue ML 329 (freely available to publish without permission).

From the tone of her mother's correspondence, Harriet absorbed much of her mother's lively personality and conversational style. In a letter to a friend in England in 1829, Mrs Blaxland wrote about the new husband of her niece, Maria: "...I hear he is a very handsome, fine young man, about twenty-eight years of age, and is designated 'The Lady Killer'—and though so young, Maria is his third wife—'an alarming distinction' you will say in the mind of a fair young bride—and so it would be but for the charm of his manners and appearance which quite bespeak the fascination for those whom he would wish to please."[104]

Harriet had leapt at the opportunity to escape parental control to live with her relatives in Kolkata but, when her three-year-old daughter fell gravely ill in India, she sent her half-way around the world to her mother. Then, when she herself fell ill, it was the care of her mother that she sought. Their relationship was strained by their proximity for over twelve years before Harriet married Dowling. Further estrangement had resulted from the inheritance disagreement between the Hogues and the Blaxlands. While Harriet described her reconciliation with her father, she made no mention of anything similar occurring with her mother. Possibly, her mother's stroke was disabling to the extent that this could not occur.

After Dowling's death, Harriet had lived in a house nearby Brougham Lodge as arranged by her step-son, Vincent Dowling, as the Lodge needed to be leased to cover expenses. However, it was likely that she was back at Brougham Lodge when she returned to Sydney in 1851. At some point, George came to reside with her, possibly due to his own financial straits, dying there in 1855.[105] Harriet, rather than her brothers, was executrix of his estate. With this duty completed, Harriet resolved to return to live permanently in England.

By the time she left in 1857, life in the colony had been changed forever through the discovery of gold in 1851. The numbers of men who headed for the goldfields compounded the labour shortages which had resulted without the steady supply of convicts. The days of squatters' privileges were over, and the lengthy financial troubles of the Newington estate were ended when it was transferred to the government as part of the Insolvent Estate of her brother, Edward James Blaxland, in 1860.

Harriet set sail in January 1857; this time by steamer—the European and Australian Royal Mail Company's steamer *Oneida* bound for the United Kingdom, by way of Marseilles and Southampton.[106] The steamer route went first to India, then across the Arabian Sea, and then via Egypt (overland, until the Suez Canal was opened in 1869) to England. This route gave Harriet the opportunity to stay with her sons for about another year before the final stage of the journey. At that time in India, British rule was challenged by the Bengal Mutiny,[107] although Harriet would have been insulated by the distance of Madras (Chennai) from the centre of unrest.

The next leg of her journey brought its own excitement as, in May 1858, she was amongst the passengers on the P & O Company steamer *Ava* which was shipwrecked, without loss of life, travelling between Madras and Marseilles.[108] Her travel documents of 1858, issued in Alexandria indicated that she was travelling with her granddaughter Kate Macdonald Ritchie (possibly a child of her younger son, Alec) as well as her "European" servant, Elizabeth Hill.[109]

A Gentleman's Daughter

20 HARRIET DOWLING'S PASSPORT, 1858

"*Passport Issued by John Green, Her Britannic Majesty's Consul at Alexandria in Egypt, to Lady Harriet Dowling, Her Granddaughter Kate Macdonald Ritchie, and a Female Servant Named Elizabeth Hill, in Order to Travel to England Via the Continent, 19 March 1858.*" Photographed by the author with permission from the collections of the State Library of NSW, Catalogue Ad 60 (freely available to publish without permission).[110]

In England, Harriet lived in Bath and, finally, in Bromley, Kent amongst her Blaxland relatives. She maintained her interest in the colony—and her own prestige—as one of the patrons of the Society for the Promotion of Female Emigration, one of the many charitable societies which sponsored the migration of respectable young women to New South Wales.[111]

At the age of seventy-one, Harriet visited Australia one last time: this time for a three-year stay, arriving late in 1871.[112] By then, her two remaining brothers, Arthur and Edward, had died—Arthur in 1866 at the age of fifty at Fordwich, and Edward in 1873 at the age of fifty-three (having established himself in Toowoomba Queensland after his financial difficulties in 1860).[113] Her daughter Eliza was a fifty-six-year-old widow following the death of her husband Charles Boydell, a leading pastoralist and magistrate in the Hunter region. Harriet's grandchildren were aged between nineteen and thirty-five, many with children of their own. James Sheen Dowling was fully occupied as senior District Court judge.[114] The other surviving Dowling children were based outside Sydney (Vincent[115] in Dungog, NSW, and Eliza[116] and Susannah[117] in Queensland).

Harriet took up residence on her own in Double Bay, advertising for a "respectable competent" cook[118] and picking up the social threads, for example, attending the Anglican Church picnic to Lithgow Valley.[119] In February 1873, she took the opportunity to travel to Bathurst to visit Marsh, her fellow passenger on her first voyage back to England. Marsh was a magistrate by then and his diary reported frequent dinners and calls during February of that year with Harriet and her travelling companion, Miss Blaxland—probably her sixty-six-year-old sister, Louisa.

Her cook may have caught wind of Harriet's intention to return to England, as Harriet was advertising in June 1873 for a replacement.[120] In August 1873, Harriet put her household goods up for auction[121] and tried to find a buyer for a painting by Marshall Claxton left to her by her brother, George. The painting depicted a diving cave at Vava'u which had been given to George by naval officer Sir Everard Home (1798–1853) in gratitude for showing him the cave.

Harriet may have provided the newspaper with the colourful note that read in part, "Our readers will doubtless remember that this extraordinary cavern is vividly described by Lord Byron in his poem 'The Island', where it is introduced as the temporary retreat of Christian and his dark-eyed Princess."[122] Unfortunately, the pitch failed to elicit a buyer and Harriet donated the painting to the Australian Museum[123] before she departing on the *Bangalore* in 1873,[124] again via Madras (Chennai).

Harriet may have found the journey fatiguing or the need for financial restraint finally caught up with her, as she made no more voyages. Taking stock of her life, she wrote her memoirs in 1875 on her return to Bath.

She lived to learn of the sad death of her elder son, Arthur Ritchie. He returned to Australia alone and in poor health from his role as Registrar of the Supreme Court of Bombay in 1876 at the age of fifty-seven. He settled in Latrobe, Tasmania and ran a small legal practice but his health problems continued. He died in Launceston Hospital of a serious bacterial infection two years later.[125]

Harriet died aged eighty-one, in Bromley, Kent, on 21st March 1881.[126] It is possible that her younger son, Alec, was with her at the time, since he was recorded as residing in London in the English Census of 1881. Her death was reported in the Home News sections in a number of newspapers in New South Wales. The Goulburn Herald added the note that her annual £200 pension would now revert to government revenue.[127]

Her two remaining sisters, Louisa and Anna, lived for a further seven years. Louisa Blaxland died in 1888, having successfully petitioned the government for permission to reside at Newington five years earlier,[128] and Anna Walker died in 1889. Harriet's younger son, Alec, lived to the age of seventy-four (died in 1896) and her daughter, Eliza, to the age of eighty-two (died in 1899).

Harriet's life had extended across the nineteenth century. The technological advances of that century showed in the duration of the trip she grew to know so well. On that first voyage, *The Brothers* left England on 17th October 1806 and arrived at Port Jackson on Friday 3rd April 1807—a journey of over five months.[129] Forty-five years later, the same journey took a little over three months and, by her last visit to Australia in 1873, she travelled by steamer and was able to go via the Suez Canal, a journey of about two months.

Her life charted the course of New South Wales from its early days as a penal colony with a population of around 5,000 to a fast-growing nation of around 750,000. Her grandchildren in Australia were part of the generation that brought about the Federation of the six separate States under a single constitution with a national parliament in 1901.[130] However, considering Harriet's account of her life and interests, if she had still been alive at the turn of the century, then I like to think it would have been the news of the latest scandals about the many mistresses of the Prince of Wales (later Edward VII) that enlivened her conversation.[131]

11 A Shared Indulgence

To introduce her memoir, Harriet referred to the changes and upheavals experienced through Europe during and after the Napoleonic Wars: "Under the influence of the prevailing domestic and mental revolution commencing with the early part of the present century, I doubt if much interest will be attached to anything in my power to describe of those early days referred to; nevertheless, there may be an attraction in the very contrast, and I will therefore indulge the simple desire of writing."

However, Harriet knew the value of her tales, having told them to her friends and family over the years, many of whom no doubt urged her to write them down. Far from situating herself at the periphery of observed events, she placed herself in the centre of her world: albeit, a narrow society shaped by position and wealth and blinkered to the hardships and aspirations of others.

Harriet might not have been the friend you sought for political wisdom or support in times of trouble, but she would have been the first person you invited to your home for a dinner party—though, if travel by sea was involved, then you might want to beware lest she decide to make her stay a long one. As for any memoirist, her writing was an act self-indulgence but, in her writing, Harriet indulged and intrigued all of us, so many generations later, by the tales she told, and the ones she left out.

Appendices

APPENDIX 1 HARRIET AND HER BROTHERS AND SISTERS

Name	Born-Died	Married	Children (male, female)
Harriet Mary Blaxland	1799-1881	1816: Alexander Macdonald Ritchie 1835: James Dowling	2m, 1f
John Marquet Blaxland	1801-1840	Unmarried	
George Blaxland	1802-1855	1834: Maria Dowling	
Anna Elizabeth Blaxland	1804-1889	1823: Thomas Walker	4m, 9f
Jane Elizabeth Blaxland	1806-1843	Unmarried	
Louisa Australia Blaxland	1807-1888	Unmarried	
Eliza Maria Blaxland	1808-1834	1832: Henry William Breton	
Edward James Blaxland	1813-1873	(date unknown): Janet Cartwright	2f
Mary Ellen Blaxland	1815-1843	1836: William Macquarie Molle	1m
Arthur Blaxland	1816-1866	1839: Elizabeth Forster	4m, 5f

APPENDIX 2 HARRIET'S RELATIVES FROM INDIA

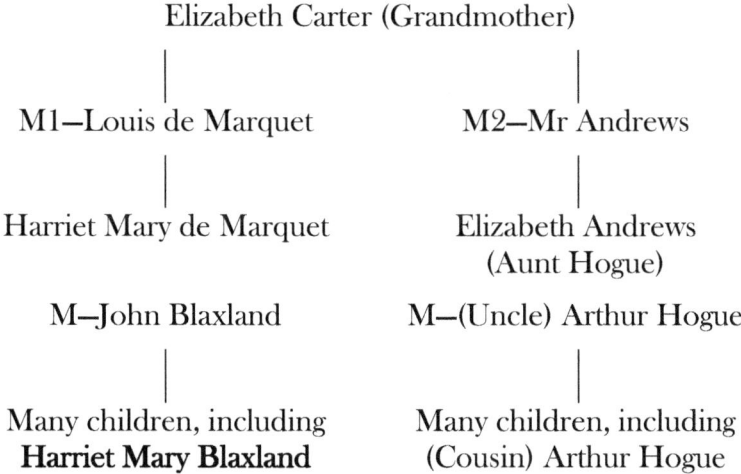

Elizabeth Carter (Grandmother)

M1—Louis de Marquet   M2—Mr Andrews

Harriet Mary de Marquet   Elizabeth Andrews
                                 (Aunt Hogue)

M—John Blaxland   M—(Uncle) Arthur Hogue

Many children, including   Many children, including
Harriet Mary Blaxland   (Cousin) Arthur Hogue

Appendix 3 Harriet's Children

Name	Born–Died	Married	Children
Elizabeth ('Eliza') Ritchie	1817–1899	1837: Charles Boydell	4m, 3f
Arthur Ritchie	1819–1878	1848-: Mary Jane Hobbs	1f*
Alexander ('Alec') Macdonald Ritchie	1821–1895	1842: Agnes Duncan** 1854: Frances Francklyne	1f*

* The number of children is uncertain.

** Verification not available and so not included in the text.

APPENDIX 4 HARRIET'S STEP-CHILDREN

(at the time of her marriage to Dowling in 1835*)

Name	Born–Died	Married	Children
Vincent Francis Woodcock Dowling	1816–1902	1849: Jane Mackay	4m, 4f
Anne Dowling	1818–1836	Unmarried	
James Sheen Dowling	1819–1902	1849: Katharine Marian Laidley	6m, 3f
Eliza Dowling	1821–1902	1842: Arthur Hodgson	
Susannah Dowling	1823–1898	1842: Charles Spencer	

*Dowling's other children by his first wife, Maria (née Sheen) were Maria (1815-1834) and four children who died in infancy: Charles (1822), Thomas William (1823-1824); Jemima (1823-1826); Henry Brougham (1828).

APPENDIX 5 SUMMARY OF EVENTS IN HARRIET'S LIFE

Year	Event
1799	Born Newington, Kent
1806	Arrived in Sydney on *The Brothers*
1814	Sailed Sydney to Kolkata on the *Eliza*
1816	Married Alexander Macdonald Ritchie, Kolkata
1817-21	Children: Eliza, Arthur, Alec
1822	Sailed to Sydney on the *John Bull*
1825	Ritchie arrived Sydney on *Mary Hope*
1826	Sailed to Kolkata on the *Katherine Stewart Forbes*
1827	Sailed to Sydney via Batavia, on the *Marquis of Lansdowne:* heard of Ritchie's death
1835	Married James Dowling at Parramatta
1844	Sir James Dowling, died aged 57 in Sydney
1845	Father, John Blaxland, died aged 77 at Newington
1847	Sailed to London on *Sir George Seymour*
1849	Sailed to Madras (Chennai) on the *Trafalgar*
1850	Arrived in Sydney on the *Vimeira*
1852	Mother, Harriet de Marquet Blaxland, died
1857	Left Sydney by steamer, *Oneida* (to India, and later to England)
1871-3	Last visit to Australia
1875	Wrote memoir in Bath, England
1881	Died in Bromley, Kent

Acknowledgements

Harriet Dowling's memoir has been of interest to her descendants over many generations and typed copies were held by family members as well as donated (along with the collection of Dowling family papers) to the Sir William Dixson Library and moved across to the State Library of New South Wales along with the rest of the collection when it was bequeathed to the State in 1952. These typed copies are located with other material in the Dowling family papers which is open for public inspection the Special Collections (see Bibliography for catalogue details). There is a handwritten note on one of those copies that the original was held by Mrs George Scott in Newcastle who was Harriet Dowling's grand-daughter, Eliza Marianne Boydell (1845-1920). In 1886 (at forty-one years of age) she married Mr George Frederick Scott (1853-1910) and they had no children. However, at the time of writing this biography, I have not been able to locate the original handwritten copy.

I owe many thanks to my brother-in-law, Gordon King (sadly, now deceased), for recognising the value of Harriet's memoir to the Blaxland story, and also to his widow, Yvonne King, for passing along the typed copy of the memoir that had been previously held by William Edward Molle (Harriet's great-great nephew). I am enormously grateful to my husband, Ian King, for helping me understand the intricacies of the Blaxland family heritage, as well as for his patience in reading numerous drafts. (Harriet's youngest brother's granddaughter, Amelia Rodd Blaxland, was the King's maternal grandmother.) My thanks are also owed to Richard Blaxland for his guidance to useful sources of family history. Thanks too for the information provided by Peter Dowling (great-great-grandson of Sir James Dowling) and for the enthusiastic interest of Michael Heath-Caldwell (distantly related to J.A. Milbourne Marsh, whose diaries are cited in this book).

I was fortunate to have Mr Santimoy Bhattacharya, retired history teacher, as my guide to Kolkata. I am grateful also to have had the support and critical input of my fellow members of the Lake Macquarie branch, Fellowship of Writers (NSW) amongst many others who have read versions of this material.

Researching the material for this biography would not have been possible without the assistance of the ever-patient librarians in the Special Collections area of the State Library of New South Wales; the extensive Australian history resources at the University of Newcastle, NSW; and, most importantly, the digital resources of Trove, supported by the National Library of Australia.

Naturally, all credit is due to the fascinating stories of Harriet, while any errors are my own.

Bibliography

Primary Sources

State Library of New South Wales

Blaxland, H. "Copy of Letter to Mrs Tilden." In *Blaxland family papers, 1837-1923*. Manuscripts, Oral History & Pictures, State Library of New South Wales, Sydney, Catalogue Ab50, 1829.

———. "Sketch of the Life of Harriott the Wife of John Blaxland the Elder, Dictated to Her Daughter Louisa Australia Blaxland, 29 May." In *Dowling family papers, 1767-1905*. Manuscripts, Oral History & Pictures, State Library of New South Wales, Catalogue DLMSQ 305, Item 5, 1848.

Blaxland, J. "Copy of John Blaxland's Note Re Title Deeds , 29 April 1828." In *Dowling family papers, 1767-1905*. Manuscripts, Oral History & Pictures, State Library of New South Wales, Sydney, Catalogue MSQ 305, 1828.

———. "Copy of John Blaxland's Will, 19 September 1844." In *Walker family papers, 1808-1933: Together with Blaxland family papers, 1780, 1797-1887*. Manuscripts, Oral History & Pictures, State Library of New South Wales, Sydney, Catalogue MLMSS 462/2, 1844.

———. "Letter, 22 May 1837, Jane Blaxland to Anna Walker (Nee Blaxland) - Transcript." (Original letter located in Manuscripts, Oral History & Pictures, State Library of New South Wales, Catalogue Ab50), http://www.sl.nsw.gov.au/stories/hunter-valley/family-life, online access confirmed 1 February 2017.

———. "Trust Deed from the Late Mr Andrews, 10th March 1810." In *Walker family papers, 1808-1933: Together with Blaxland family papers, 1780, 1797-1887*. Manuscripts, Oral

History & Pictures, State Library of New South Wales, Sydney, Catalogue MLMSS 462/3, 1810.

Dowling, H. "Memoir of the Early Life of Harriott Mary Dowling Nee Blaxland: Or Sketches of India and Australia in Old Times." In *Dowling family papers 1767-1905*: Manuscripts, Oral History & Pictures, State Library of New South Wales, Catalogue DLMSQ 305, Item 5, 1875.

Dowling, J. "Letter to His Son, James Sheen Dowling, Dated 17 March." In *Dowling family papers, 1767-1905*. Manuscripts, Oral History & Pictures, State Library of New South Wales, Sydney, Catalogue DLMS SQ 305, 1841.

Hansard & Papers, Legislative Council of New South Wales. "Lady Dowling's Pension." in *Dowling family papers*, 1767-1905. Manuscripts, Oral History & Pictures, State Library of New South Wales, Sydney, Catalogue DLMSQ 305, Item 5, 1848.

Her Britannic Majesty's Consul. "Passport Issued by John Green, Her Britannic Majesty's Consul at Alexandria in Egypt, to Lady Harriet Dowling, Her Granddaughter Kate Macdonald Ritchie, and a Female Servant Named Elizabeth Hill, in Order to Travel to England Via the Continent, 19 March 1858." Manuscripts, Oral History & Pictures, State Library of New South Wales, State Library of NSW, Catalogue Ad60, 1858.

von Hügel, C. "Letter to Jane Blaxland, 2nd March." In *Walker family papers, 1808-1933: together with Blaxland family papers, 1780, 1797-1887*: Manuscripts, Oral History & Pictures, State Library of New South Wales, Catalogue MLMSS462, Box 2, 1840.

Walker, A.E. "Letter to Her Sisters Jane and Louisa Blaxland, 18th November." In *Walker family papers, 1808-1933: together with Blaxland family papers, 1780, 1797-1887*. Manuscripts,

Oral History & Pictures, State Library of New South Wales, Sydney, Catalogue MLMSS 462 1(3), 1835.

Walker, A.F. "Walker Family: Family Traditions and Personal Recollections (Unpublished Papers, Copied after the Death of the Author)." In *Walker family papers, 1808-1933: together with Blaxland family papers, 1780, 1797-1887*: Manuscripts, Oral History & Pictures, State Library of NSW, Catalogue MLMSS 462, Box 1, 1913.

State Records, New South Wales

Baxter, C. "Musters of New South Wales and Norfolk Island 1805-1806." Australian Biographical and Genealogical Record (Biographical Database of Australia), http://www.bda-online.org.au/files/MC1805_Muster.pdf, online access confirmed 1 February 2017.

Bladen, F.M., ed. *Historical Records of New South Wales, Bligh and Macquarie, 1809-1811* Vol. 7. Sydney, NSW: Government Printer (CD - Gould Genealogy & History), 1901.

———, ed. *Historical Records of New South Wales, King and Bligh, 1806-1808* Vol. 6. Sydney, NSW: Government Printer (CD - Gould Genealogy & History), 1898.

Newspapers

Australian Town and Country Journal. "Shipping Arrivals, December 28." *Australian Town and Country Journal (NSW, 1870-1907)*, Saturday 30 December 1871, 27.

Goulburn Herald. "(Lady Dowling's Death)." *Goulburn Herald (NSW 1881-1907)*, 1881, 2.

Ipswich Herald and General Advertiser. "Queensland News (by Electric Telegraph; from Our Correspondent)." *Ipswich Herald and General Advertiser (QLD: 1861-1908)*, Tuesday 18 October 1898, 5.

Launceston Courier. "Wreck of the Clonmel Steam Ship." *Launceston Courier (Tas: 1840-1843)*, Monday 18 January 1841, 2.

Launceston Examiner. "Deaths: Arthur Macdonald Ritchie." *Launceston Examiner (Tas: 1842-1899)*, Saturday 31 August 1878, 2.

———. "Marriages: Arthur Madonald Ritchie." *Launceston Examiner (Tas: 1842-1899)*, Wednesday 29 August 1849, 6.

Salmon, M. "Some Australian Pioneers: Hon. John Blaxland." *Sunday Times (Sydney, NSW: 1895-1930)*, Sunday 12 June 1910, 19.

Simson, D.C. "Loss of the Clonmel." *The Courier (Hobart, Tas: 1840-1859)*, Tuesday 19 January 1841, 2.

Solomon. "Singleton of Other Days: Its People and Affairs." *Singleton Argus (NSW: 1880 - 1954)*, Friday 22 February 1935, 8.

The Maitland Mercury & Hunter River General Advertiser. "Death Notice, Harriet, Relict of the Late John Blaxland Esq." *The Maitland Mercury & Hunter River General Advertiser*, Saturday 10 January 1852.

———. "Death of Chief Justice." *The Maitland Mercury & Hunter River General Advertiser*, Saturday 5 October 1844.

The Sydney Gazette and New South Wales Advertiser. "Arrivals." *The Sydney Gazette and New South Wales Advertiser (NSW: 1803-1842)*, Thursday 27 September 1838, 2.

———. "Highway Robberies." *Sydney Gazette and New South Wales Advertiser (NSW: 1803-1842)*, Thursday 22 April 1830, 2.

———. "(No Title: The Gentlemen of the Colony...)." *The Sydney Gazette and New South Wales Advertiser (NSW: 1803 - 1842)*, Thursday 1 September 1825, 2.

———. "Notice." *The Sydney Gazette and New South Wales Advertiser (NSW: 1803 - 1842)*, Saturday, 17 July 1813, 1.

———. "Ship News." *The Sydney Gazette and New South Wales Advertiser (NSW: 1803 - 1842)*, Sunday 5 April 1807, 1.

———. "Ship News." *The Sydney Gazette and New South Wales Advertiser (NSW: 1803 - 1842)*, Saturday 13 August 1814, 2.

———. "Sydney Gazette." *The Sydney Gazette and New South Wales Advertiser (NSW: 1803 - 1842)*, Wednesday 19 April 1815, 2.

———. "Tasmanian News: Hobart Town Gazette." *The Sydney Gazette and New South Wales Advertiser (NSW: 1803 - 1842)*, Thursday 25 January 1827, 3.

The Sydney Mail and New South Wales Advertiser. "Anglican Church Conference: Picnic to Lithgow Valley." *The Sydney Mail and New South Wales Advertiser (NSW: 1871-1912)*, Saturday 19 October 1872, 489.

The Sydney Morning Herald. "Advertising: Public Auction." *Sydney Morning Herald (NSW: 1842-1954)*, Friday 8 August 1873, 7.

———. "Advertising: Wanted." *Sydney Morning Herald (NSW: 1842-1954)*, Wednesday 17 January 1872, 8.

———. "Advertising: Wanted." *Sydney Morning Herald (NSW: 1842-1954)*, Thursday 19 June 1873, 8.

———. "The Chief Justice." *The Sydney Morning Herald (NSW: 1842-1954)*, Friday 23 August 1844, 2.

———. "Death of Mr Vincent Dowling." *The Sydney Morning Herald (NSW: 1842-1954)*, Thursday 25 December 1902, 4.

———. "Death of the Chief Justice." *The Sydney Morning Herald (NSW: 1842-1954)*, Saturday 28 September 1844, 2.

———. "Deaths (George Blaxland)." *The Sydney Morning Herald (NSW: 1842-1954)*, Thursday 11 October 1855 1855, 6.

———. "Deaths (Louisa Australia Blaxland)." *The Sydney Morning Herald (NSW: 1842-1954)*, Saturday 4 August 1888, 1.

———. "Died (John Blaxland)." *The Sydney Morning Herald (NSW: 1842-1954)*, Wednesday 6 August 1845, 3.

———. "From the Home News: Female Emigration to Australia." *Sydney Morning Herald (NSW: 1842-1954)*, Tuesday 27 January 1863.

———. "The Great Protest Meeting." *The Sydney Morning Herald (NSW: 1842-1954)*, Tuesday 12 June 1849, 2.

———. "Lady Dowling." *The Sydney Morning Herald (NSW: 1842-1954)*, Monday 24 December 1849, 2.

———. "List of Donations to the Australian Museum During August and September 1873." *Sydney Morning Herald (NSW: 1842-1954)*, Monday 6 October 1873, 3.

———. "Mails by the European and Australian Royal Mail Company's Steamer Oneida." *The Sydney Morning Herald (NSW: 1842-1954)*, Thursday 22 January 1857, 4.

———. "Marriages (Alexander Macdonald Ritchie)." *The Sydney Morning Herald (NSW: 1842-1954)*, Saturday 28 January 1854, 5.

———. "Miss Blaxland's Petition." *The Sydney Morning Herald (NSW: 1842-1954)*, Wednesday 28 November 1883, 2.

———. "News of the Day (Lady Dowling's Death)." *Sydney Morning Herald (NSW: 1842-1954)*, Saturday 21 May 1881, 5.

———. "One of Claxton's Pictures." *Sydney Morning Herald (NSW: 1842-1954)*, Thursday 14 August 1873, 4.

———. "Pensions to Ladies Forbes and Dowling." *The Sydney Morning Herald (NSW: 1842 - 1954)*, Friday 29 May 1846, 2.

———. "Royal Mail Notice." *Sydney Morning Herald (NSW: 1842-1954)*, Tuesday 2 December 1873, 4.

———. "Shipping Intelligence: Arrivals." *The Sydney Morning Herald (NSW: 1842-1954)*, Tuesday 29 April 1851, 2.

———. "The Wrecked P. and O. Company's Steamer Ava (from the Ceylon Observer)." *The Sydney Morning Herald (NSW: 1842-1954)*, Saturday 1st May 1858, 4.

Published primary sources

de Bougainville, H.Y.P.P. *The Governor's Noble Guest: Hyacinthe De Bougainville's Account of Port Jackson, 1825.* Translated by M.S. Riviere. Carlton, Vic: Melbourne University Press, 1999.

Dowling, J.S. *Reminiscences of a Colonial Judge*. Leichhardt, NSW: Federation Press, 1996.

Marsh, J.A.M. "Diary of John Augustus Milbourne Marsh (1819-1891): 1847 (Transcribed from Betty Harrison Family Archives, by Michael Heath-Caldwell, Brisbane 2009)." http://www.jjhc.info/marshjohnaugustusmilbourne1891diary1847.htm, online access confirmed 1 February 2017.

von Hügel, C. *New Holland Journal, November 1833 - October 1834 (Translated and Edited by Dymphna Clark)*. Melbourne, Vic: Melbourne University Press, 1994.

Secondary Sources

Published secondary sources

Alexander, A. *The Ambitions of Jane Franklin: Victorian Lady Adventurer*. Sydney, NSW: Allen & Unwin, 2013.

Allars, K.G. "Burton, Sir William Westbrooke (1794-1888)." Australian Dictionary of Biography, National Centre of Biography, Australian National University, http://adb.anu.edu.au/biography/burton-sir-william-westbrooke-1857, published first in hardcopy 1966, online access confirmed 1 February 2017.

Australian Dictionary of Biography. "O Connell, Sir Maurice Charles (1768-1848)." Australian Dictionary of Biography, National Centre of Biography, Australian National University, http://adb.anu.edu.au/biography/oconnell-sir-maurice-charles-2517, published first in hardcopy 1967, online access confirmed 1 February 2017.

Bennett, J.M. *Sir James Dowling: Second Chief Justice of New South Wales 1837-1844 (Foreword, Bruce Mansfield)*. Annandale, NSW: Federation Press, 2001.

Blaxland, P. *The Gentlemen Settlers: A Romance of Colonial Australia.* Sydney, NSW: Angus & Robertson, 1975.

Camden, W. "Kent." In *Britannia or a chorographical description of Great Britain and Ireland, together with the adjacent islands* Adelaide, SA: University of Adelaide, 1722. https://ebooks.adelaide.edu.au/c/camden/william/britannia-gibson-1722/part49.html, online access confirmed 1 February 2017.

Castle, T.D., and B. Kercher. *The Dowling Legacy: Foundations of an Australian Legal Culture 1828-1844.* Sydney, NSW: The Francis Forbes Society for Legal History, 2005.

Chaudhuri, K.N., ed. *The Economic Development of India under the East India Company 1814-58: A Selection of Contemporary Writings.* Cambridge, UK: Cambridge University Press, 1971.

Cochrane, P. *Colonial Ambition: Foundations of Australian Democracy.* Melbourne, Vic: Melbourne University Press, 2006.

Conway, J. "Blaxland, Gregory (1778-1853)." *Australian Dictionary of Biography*, no. 1 - First published in hardcopy in Australian Dictionary of Biography, Volume 1, Melbourne University Press, 1966 (1966). http://adb.anu.edu.au/biography/blaxland-gregory-1795, published first in hardcopy 1966, online access confirmed 1 February 2017.

Curran, S. "Women Readers, Women Writers." In *The Cambridge Companion to British Romanticism*, edited by S. Curran, 169-86. Cambridge, UK: Cambridge University Press, 2010.

Currey, C.H. "Dowling, Sir James (1787-1844)." Australian Dictionary of Biography, National Centre of Biography, Australian National University, http://adb.anu.edu.au/biography/dowling-sir-james-1989, published first in hardcopy 1966, online access confirmed 1 February 2017.

Dalrymple, W. *White Mughals: Love and Betrayal in Eighteenth-Century India.* New York, NY: Viking, 2003.

Dowling, A.R. "Dowling, James Sheen (1819-1902)." National Centre of Biography, Australian National University, http://adb.anu.edu.au/biography/dowling-james-sheen-3436, published first in hardcopy 1972, online access confirmed 1 February 2017.

Dyer, C. *The French Explorers and Sydney: 1788-1831.* St Lucia, QLD: University of Queensland Press, 2009.

Dyster, B. *Servant and Master: Building and Running the Grand Houses of Sydney 1788-1850.* Kensington, NSW: New South Wales University Press, 1989.

Hainsworth, D.R. "Lord, Simeon (1771-1840)." Australian Dictionary of Biography, National Centre of Biography, Australian National University, http://adb.anu.edu.au/biography/lord-simeon-2371, published first in hardcopy 1967, online access confirmed 1 February 2017.

Harrison, A.J. "Tony Harrison's Site: Samuel Wright and His Uncle." http://www.users.on.net/~ahvem/page3/page11/page60/page68/page68.html, online access confirmed 1 February 2017.

Haskins, V.K., and C. Lowrie. "Introduction: Decolonizing Domestic Service - Introducing a New Agenda." In *Colonization and Domestic Service: Historical and Contemporary Perspectives*, edited by V.K. Haskins and C. Lowrie, pp. 1-18. Hoboken, NJ: Taylor and Francis, 2014.

Houison, J.K.S. *John and Gregory Blaxland, Paper Read before the Royal Australian Historical Society, October 29.* Sydney, NSW: Royal Australian Historical Society, 1935.

Irving, T.H. "Blaxland, John (1769-1845)." Australian Dictionary of Biography, National Centre of Biography, Australian National University, http://adb.anu.edu.au/biography/blaxland-john-1796, published first in hardcopy 1967, online access confirmed 1 February 2017.

James, L. *Raj: The Making and Unmaking of British India.* New York, NY: St Martin's Press, 1998.

Karskens, G. *The Colony: A History of Early Sydney.* Sydney, NSW: Allen & Unwin, 2010.

Kelly, G. *English Fiction of the Romantic Period, 1789-1830.* London, UK: Longman, 1989.

Kercher, B. *Unruly Child: A History of Law in Australia.* Sydney: Allen & Unwin, 2014.

Kumagi, Yukihisa. "Defending the Monopoly: The East India Company, 1790s-1830s." Chap. 1 In *Breaking into the Monopoly: Provincial Merchants and Manufacturers' Campaigns for Access to the Asian Market, 1790-1833*, 7-32. Leiden, The Netherlands: Koninklijke Brill NV, 2012.

Kyle, N. *Her Natural Destiny: The Education of Women in New South Wales.* Kensington, NSW: New South Wales University Press, 1986.

Levine, P. *The British Empire: Sunrise to Sunset.* Harlow, UK: Pearson Longman, 2007.

Mani, L. *Contentious Traditions: The Debate on Sati in Colonial India.* Berkeley, CA: University of California Press, 1998.

Markovits, C. *Merchants, Traders, Entrepreneurs: Indian Business in the Colonial Era.* Basingstoke, UK: Palgrave Macmillan ebooks, 2008.

Morris, S. *Rolling Down the Years with the Blaxlands and the Parramores.* Wagga Wagga, NSW: Sherry Morris, 1993.

Neal, D. *The Rule of Law in a Penal Colony: Law and Power in Early New South Wales.* Cambridge, UK: Cambridge University Press, 1991.

O'Connor, D. *The Chaplains of the East India Company, 1601-1858.* London, UK: Continuum International Publishing, 2011.

Obituaries Australia. "Hodgson, Lady Eliza (1821-1902)." National Centre of Biography, Australian National University, http://oa.anu.edu.au/obituary/hodgson-lady-eliza-1154, online access confirmed 1 February 2017.

Olsen, P. *Collecting Ladies: Ferdinand Von Mueller and Women Botanical Articles.* Sydney, NSW: National Library of Australia, 2013.

Project Canterbury. "Anglicanism on the Indian Subcontinent." http://anglicanhistory.org/india/, online access confirmed 1 February 2017.

Rose, J. *Zoroastrianism: An Introduction.* New York, NY: L.B. Tauris & Co., 2011.

Roxburgh, R. *Early Colonial Houses of New South Wales.* Sydney, NSW: Ure Smith, 1974.

Russell, P. *This Errant Lady: Jane Franklin's Overland Journey to Port Phillip and Sydney, 1839.* Canberra, ACT: National Library of Australia, 2002.

Shaw, A.G.L. "Bligh, William (1754-1817)." Australian Dictionary of Biography, National Centre of Biography, Australian National University, http://adb.anu.edu.au/biography/bligh-william-1797, published first in hardcopy 1966, online access confirmed 1 February 2017.

Theobald, M.R. *Knowing Women: Origins of Women's Education in Nineteenth-Century Australia.* Cambridge, UK: Cambridge University Press, 1996.

Webster, A. *The Richest East India Merchant: The Life and Business of John Palmer of Calcutta 1767-1836.* Woodbridge, UK: Boydell Press, 2007.

———. *The Twilight of the East India Company: The Evolution of Anglo-Asian Commerce and Politics.* Woodbridge: Boydell & Brewer, 2009.

Weintraub, S. "The King's Loose Box: Edward VII as Priapic Prince of Wales." *English Literature in Transition* 60, no. 1 (2017): 3-15.

Westrip, J., and P. Holroyde. *Colonial Cousins: A Surprising History of Connections between India and Australia.* Kent Town, South Australia: Wakefield Press, 2010.

Wickes, H.L. *Regiments of Foot: A Historical Record of All the Foot Regiments of the British Army.* Berkshire: Osprey, 1974.

Wood, G.H. "Changes in Average Wages in New South Wales, 1823-98." *Journal of the Royal Statistical Society* 64, no. 2 (1901): 327-35.

Wood, W.A. *Dawn in the Valley: The Story of Settlement in the Hunter River Valley to 1833.* Sydney, NSW: Wentworth Books, 1972.

Unpublished secondary sources

Bubacz, B.M. "The Female and Male Orphan Schools in New South Wales 1801-1850." Doctor of Philosophy, University of Sydney, 2007.

Works Cited

―――――――――――――

[1] H. Dowling, "Memoir of the Early Life of Harriott Mary Dowling Nee Blaxland: Or Sketches of India and Australia in Old Times," in *Dowling family papers 1767-1905* (Manuscripts, Oral History & Pictures, State Library of New South Wales, Catalogue DLMSQ 305, Item 5, 1875).

[2] F.M. Bladen, ed. *Historical Records of New South Wales, King and Bligh, 1806-1808*, vol. 6 (Sydney, NSW: Government Printer (CD - Gould Genealogy & History), 1898), p. 114.

[3] *Historical Records of New South Wales, Bligh and Macquarie, 1809-1811*, vol. 7 (Sydney, NSW: Government Printer (CD - Gould Genealogy & History), 1901), pp. 223-4.

[4] A.G.L. Shaw, "Bligh, William (1754-1817)," Australian Dictionary of Biography, National Centre of Biography, Australian National University, http://adb.anu.edu.au/biography/bligh-william-1797, published first in hardcopy 1966, online access confirmed 1 February 2017.

[5] Bladen, *Historical Records of New South Wales, King and Bligh, 1806-1808*, p. 379.

[6] J.K.S. Houison, *John and Gregory Blaxland, Paper Read before the Royal Australian Historical Society, October 29* (Sydney, NSW: Royal Australian Historical Society, 1935).

[7] D.R. Hainsworth, "Lord, Simeon (1771-1840)," Australian Dictionary of Biography, National Centre of Biography, Australian National University, http://adb.anu.edu.au/biography/lord-simeon-2371, published first in hardcopy 1967, online access confirmed 1 February 2017.

[8] T.H. Irving, "Blaxland, John (1769-1845)," ibid. http://adb.anu.edu.au/biography/blaxland-john-1796, published first in hardcopy 1967, online access confirmed 1 February 2017.

⁹ For overview, see D. Neal, *The Rule of Law in a Penal Colony: Law and Power in Early New South Wales* (Cambridge, UK: Cambridge University Press, 1991).

¹⁰ A.F. Walker, "Walker Family: Family Traditions and Personal Recollections (Unpublished Papers, Copied after the Death of the Author)," in *Walker family papers, 1808-1933: together with Blaxland family papers, 1780, 1797-1887* (Manuscripts, Oral History & Pictures, State Library of NSW, Catalogue MLMSS 462, Box 1, 1913).

¹¹ M. Salmon, "Some Australian Pioneers: Hon. John Blaxland," *Sunday Times (Sydney, NSW: 1895-1930)*, Sunday 12 June 1910.

¹² W. Camden, "Kent," *Britannia or a chorographical description of Great Britain and Ireland, together with the adjacent islands* (Adelaide, SA: University of Adelaide, 1722), https://ebooks.adelaide.edu.au/c/camden/william/britannia-gibson-1722/part49.html, online access confirmed 1 February 2017.

¹³ Bladen, *Historical Records of New South Wales, King and Bligh, 1806-1808*, pp. 434-5.

¹⁴ *Historical Records of New South Wales, Bligh and Macquarie, 1809-1811*, pp. 227-8.

¹⁵ G. Karskens, *The Colony: A History of Early Sydney* (Sydney, NSW: Allen & Unwin, 2010), pp. 212-3.

¹⁶ C. Baxter, "Musters of New South Wales and Norfolk Island 1805-1806," Australian Biographical and Genealogical Record (Biographical Database of Australia), http://www.bda-online.org.au/files/MC1805_Muster.pdf, online access confirmed 1 February 2017.

¹⁷ B.M. Bubacz, "The Female and Male Orphan Schools in New South Wales 1801-1850" (Doctor of Philosophy, University of Sydney, 2007).

¹⁸ V.K. Haskins and C. Lowrie, "Introduction: Decolonizing Domestic Service - Introducing a New Agenda," in *Colonization and Domestic Service: Historical and Contemporary Perspectives*, ed. V.K. Haskins and C. Lowrie (Hoboken, NJ: Taylor and Francis, 2014), pp. 1-18.

¹⁹ Karskens, pp. 98-115.

[20] Bladen, *Historical Records of New South Wales, Bligh and Macquarie, 1809-1811*, pp. 227-8.

[21] S. Morris, *Rolling Down the Years with the Blaxlands and the Parramores* (Wagga Wagga, NSW: Sherry Morris, 1993), p. 17.

[22] The Sydney Gazette and New South Wales Advertiser, "Notice," *The Sydney Gazette and New South Wales Advertiser (NSW: 1803 - 1842)*, Saturday, 17 July 1813.

[23] Morris, p. 18.

[24] M.R. Theobald, *Knowing Women: Origins of Women's Education in Nineteenth-Century Australia* (Cambridge, UK: Cambridge University Press, 1996), pp. 14-5.

[25] N. Kyle, *Her Natural Destiny: The Education of Women in New South Wales* (Kensington, NSW: New South Wales University Press, 1986), pp. 1-9.

[26] P. Olsen, *Collecting Ladies: Ferdinand Von Mueller and Women Botanical Articles* (Sydney, NSW: National Library of Australia, 2013), pp. 115-37.

[27] J. Conway, "Blaxland, Gregory (1778-1853)," *Australian Dictionary of Biography*, no. 1 - First published in hardcopy in Australian Dictionary of Biography, Volume 1, Melbourne University Press, 1966 (1966), http://adb.anu.edu.au/biography/blaxland-gregory-1795, published first in hardcopy 1966, online access confirmed 1 February 2017.

[28] H.L. Wickes, *Regiments of Foot: A Historical Record of All the Foot Regiments of the British Army* (Berkshire: Osprey, 1974), pp. 102-3.

[29] For a fictionalised rendition of Harriet de Marquet's stories of India, see P. Blaxland, *The Gentlemen Settlers: A Romance of Colonial Australia* (Sydney, NSW: Angus & Robertson, 1975).

[30] H. Blaxland, "Sketch of the Life of Harriott the Wife of John Blaxland the Elder, Dictated to Her Daughter Louisa Australia Blaxland, 29 May," in *Dowling family papers, 1767-1905* (Manuscripts, Oral History & Pictures, State Library of New South Wales, Catalogue DLMSQ 305, Item 5, 1848).

[31] Walker.

[32] J. Blaxland, "Trust Deed from the Late Mr Andrews, 10th March 1810," in *Walker family papers, 1808-1933: Together with Blaxland family papers, 1780, 1797-1887* (Manuscripts, Oral History & Pictures, State Library of New South Wales, Sydney, Catalogue MLMSS 462/31810).

[33] The Sydney Gazette and New South Wales Advertiser, "Ship News," *The Sydney Gazette and New South Wales Advertiser (NSW: 1803 - 1842)*, Saturday 13 August 1814.

[34] "Sydney Gazette," *The Sydney Gazette and New South Wales Advertiser (NSW: 1803 - 1842)*, Wednesday 19 April 1815.

[35] Ibid.

[36] S. Curran, "Women Readers, Women Writers," in *The Cambridge Companion to British Romanticism*, ed. S. Curran (Cambridge, UK: Cambridge University Press, 2010), pp. 169-86.

[37] G. Kelly, *English Fiction of the Romantic Period, 1789-1830* (London, UK: Longman, 1989), pp. 43-5.

[38] P. Levine, *The British Empire: Sunrise to Sunset* (Harlow, UK: Pearson Longman, 2007), pp. 69-74.

[39] R. Roxburgh, *Early Colonial Houses of New South Wales* (Sydney, NSW: Ure Smith, 1974), pp. 166-87.

[40] For a summary of the relationship between the East India Company, agency houses, and the native merchants, see Yukihisa Kumagi, "Defending the Monopoly: The East India Company, 1790s-1830s," in *Breaking into the Monopoly: Provincial Merchants and Manufacturers' Campaigns for Access to the Asian Market, 1790-1833* (Leiden, The Netherlands: Koninklijke Brill NV, 2012), pp. 7-32.

[41] L. Mani, *Contentious Traditions: The Debate on Sati in Colonial India* (Berkeley, CA: University of California Press, 1998), pp. 17-9.

[42] D. O'Connor, *The Chaplains of the East India Company, 1601-1858* (London, UK: Continuum International Publishing, 2011), pp. 119-44.

[43] Project Canterbury, "Anglicanism on the Indian Subcontinent," http://anglicanhistory.org/india/, online access confirmed 1 February 2017.

[44] A. Webster, *The Twilight of the East India Company: The Evolution of Anglo-Asian Commerce and Politics* (Woodbridge: Boydell & Brewer, 2009), pp. 110-43.

[45] W. Dalrymple, *White Mughals: Love and Betrayal in Eighteenth-Century India* (New York, NY: Viking, 2003), pp. 94-96.

[46] Walker.

[47] Ibid.

[48] Levine, p. 74.

[49] C. Dyer, *The French Explorers and Sydney: 1788-1831* (St Lucia, QLD: University of Queensland Press, 2009), pp. 98-140.

[50] H.Y.P.P. de Bougainville, *The Governor's Noble Guest: Hyacinthe De Bougainville's Account of Port Jackson, 1825*, trans. M.S. Riviere (Carlton, Vic: Melbourne University Press, 1999), pp. 108-83.

[51] The Sydney Gazette and New South Wales Advertiser, "(No Title: The Gentlemen of the Colony...)," *The Sydney Gazette and New South Wales Advertiser (NSW: 1803 - 1842)*, Thursday 1 September 1825.

[52] A.J. Harrison, "Tony Harrison's Site: Samuel Wright and His Uncle," http://www.users.on.net/~ahvem/page3/page11/page60/page68/page68.html, online access confirmed 1 February 2017.

[53] Levine, pp. 69-74.

[54] A. Webster, *The Richest East India Merchant: The Life and Business of John Palmer of Calcutta 1767-1836* (Woodbridge, UK: Boydell Press, 2007), pp. 110-43.

[55] K.N. Chaudhuri, ed. *The Economic Development of India under the East India Company 1814-58: A Selection of Contemporary Writings* (Cambridge, UK: Cambridge University Press, 1971), pp. 17-21.

[56] J. Westrip and P. Holroyde, *Colonial Cousins: A Surprising History of Connections between India and Australia* (Kent Town, South Australia: Wakefield Press, 2010), p. 78.

[57] J. Rose, *Zoroastrianism: An Introduction* (New York, NY: L.B. Tauris & Co., 2011), pp. xvii-xxiv.

[58] The Sydney Gazette and New South Wales Advertiser, "Tasmanian News: Hobart Town Gazette," *The Sydney Gazette and New South Wales Advertiser (NSW: 1803 - 1842)*, Thursday 25 January 1827.

[59] P. Russell, *This Errant Lady: Jane Franklin's Overland Journey to Port Phillip and Sydney, 1839* (Canberra, ACT: National Library of Australia, 2002), p. 253.

[60] W.A. Wood, *Dawn in the Valley: The Story of Settlement in the Hunter River Valley to 1833* (Sydney, NSW: Wentworth Books, 1972), p. 262.

[61] B. Dyster, *Servant and Master: Building and Running the Grand Houses of Sydney 1788-1850* (Kensington, NSW: New South Wales University Press, 1989), p. 144.

[62] B. Kercher, *Unruly Child: A History of Law in Australia* (Sydney: Allen & Unwin, 2014), p. 70.

[63] The Sydney Gazette and New South Wales Advertiser, "Highway Robberies," *Sydney Gazette and New South Wales Advertiser (NSW: 1803-1842)*, Thursday 22 April 1830.

[64] Ibid.

[65] J. Dowling, "Letter to His Son, James Sheen Dowling, Dated 17 March," in *Dowling family papers, 1767-1905* (Manuscripts, Oral History & Pictures, State Library of New South Wales, Sydney, Catalogue DLMS SQ 3051841).

[66] C. von Hügel, *New Holland Journal, November 1833 - October 1834 (Translated and Edited by Dymphna Clark)* (Melbourne, Vic: Melbourne University Press, 1994), pp. 327-96.

[67] "Letter to Jane Blaxland, 2nd March," in *Walker family papers, 1808-1933: together with Blaxland family papers, 1780, 1797-1887* (Manuscripts, Oral History & Pictures, State Library of New South Wales, Catalogue MLMSS462, Box 2, 1840).

[68] A.E. Walker, "Letter to Her Sisters Jane and Louisa Blaxland, 18th November,"ibid. (Manuscripts, Oral History & Pictures, State Library of New South Wales, Sydney, Catalogue MLMSS 462 1(3)1835).

[69] The Maitland Mercury & Hunter River General Advertiser, "Death of Chief Justice," *The Maitland Mercury & Hunter River General Advertiser*, Saturday 5 October 1844.

[70] J.S. Dowling, *Reminiscences of a Colonial Judge* (Leichhardt, NSW: Federation Press, 1996), p. 9.

[71] J.M. Bennett, *Sir James Dowling: Second Chief Justice of New South Wales 1837-1844 (Foreword, Bruce Mansfield)* (Annandale, NSW: Federation Press, 2001), p. 5.

[72] Ibid., p. 3.

[73] T.D. Castle and B. Kercher, *The Dowling Legacy: Foundations of an Australian Legal Culture 1828-1844* (Sydney, NSW: The Francis Forbes Society for Legal History, 2005), p. 13.

[74] C.H. Currey, "Dowling, Sir James (1787-1844)," Australian Dictionary of Biography, National Centre of Biography, Australian National University, http://adb.anu.edu.au/biography/dowling-sir-james-1989, published first in hardcopy 1966, online access confirmed 1 February 2017.

[75] Russell.

[76] Australian Dictionary of Biography, "O Connell, Sir Maurice Charles (1768-1848)," Australian Dictionary of Biography, National Centre of Biography, Australian National University, http://adb.anu.edu.au/biography/oconnell-sir-maurice-charles-2517, published first in hardcopy 1967, online access confirmed 1 February 2017.

[77] For a recent account of her travels, see A. Alexander, *The Ambitions of Jane Franklin: Victorian Lady Adventurer* (Sydney, NSW: Allen & Unwin, 2013).

[78] J. Blaxland, "Letter, 22 May 1837, Jane Blaxland to Anna Walker (Nee Blaxland) - Transcript," (Original letter located in Manuscripts, Oral History & Pictures, State Library of New South Wales, Catalogue Ab50), http://www.sl.nsw.gov.au/stories/hunter-valley/family-life, online access confirmed 1 February 2017.

[79] Dowling.

[80] The Sydney Gazette and New South Wales Advertiser, "Arrivals," *The Sydney Gazette and New South Wales Advertiser (NSW: 1803-1842)*, Thursday 27 September 1838.

[81] Dowling.

[82] Launceston Courier, "Wreck of the Clonmel Steam Ship," *Launceston Courier (Tas: 1840-1843)*, Monday 18 January 1841.

[83] D.C. Simson, "Loss of the Clonmel," *The Courier (Hobart, Tas: 1840-1859)*, Tuesday 19 January 1841.

[84] The Sydney Morning Herald, "The Great Protest Meeting," *The Sydney Morning Herald (NSW: 1842-1954)*, Tuesday 12 June 1849.

[85] "Death of the Chief Justice," *The Sydney Morning Herald (NSW: 1842-1954)*, Saturday 28 September 1844.

[86] "The Chief Justice," *The Sydney Morning Herald (NSW: 1842-1954)*, Friday 23 August 1844.

[87] Ibid.

[88] K.G. Allars, "Burton, Sir William Westbrooke (1794-1888)," Australian Dictionary of Biography, National Centre of Biography, Australian National University, http://adb.anu.edu.au/biography/burton-sir-william-westbrooke-1857, published first in hardcopy 1966, online access confirmed 1 February 2017.

[89] Irving.

[90] The Sydney Morning Herald, "Died (John Blaxland)," *The Sydney Morning Herald (NSW: 1842-1954)*, Wednesday 6 August 1845.

[91] J. Blaxland, "Copy of John Blaxland's Will, 19 September 1844," in *Walker family papers, 1808-1933: Together with Blaxland family papers, 1780, 1797-1887* (Manuscripts, Oral History & Pictures, State Library of New South Wales, Sydney, Catalogue MLMSS 462/21844).

[92] Morris, p. 29.

[93] G.H. Wood, "Changes in Average Wages in New South Wales, 1823-98," *Journal of the Royal Statistical Society* 64, no. 2 (1901).

[94] The Sydney Morning Herald, "Pensions to Ladies Forbes and Dowling," *The Sydney Morning Herald (NSW: 1842 - 1954)*, Friday 29 May 1846.

[95] J.A.M. Marsh, "Diary of John Augustus Milbourne Marsh (1819-1891): 1847 (Transcribed from Betty Harrison Family Archives, by Michael Heath-Caldwell, Brisbane 2009)," http://www.jjhc.info/marshjohnaugustusmilbourne1891diary1847.htm, online access confirmed 1 February 2017.

[96] Legislative Council of New South Wales Hansard & Papers, "Lady Dowling's Pension," (in *Dowling family papers*, 1767-1905. Manuscripts, Oral History & Pictures, State Library of New South Wales, Sydney, Catalogue DLMSQ 305, Item 51848).

[97] Launceston Examiner, "Marriages: Arthur Madonald Ritchie," *Launceston Examiner (Tas: 1842-1899)*, Wednesday 29 August 1849.

[98] The Sydney Morning Herald, "Marriages (Alexander Macdonald Ritchie)," *The Sydney Morning Herald (NSW: 1842-1954)*, Saturday 28 January 1854.

[99] "Lady Dowling," *The Sydney Morning Herald (NSW: 1842-1954)*, Monday 24 December 1849.

[100] "Shipping Intelligence: Arrivals," *The Sydney Morning Herald (NSW: 1842-1954)*, Tuesday 29 April 1851.

[101] The Maitland Mercury & Hunter River General Advertiser, "Death Notice, Harriet, Relict of the Late John Blaxland Esq," *The Maitland Mercury & Hunter River General Advertiser*, Saturday 10 January 1852.

[102] Olsen, pp. 115-37.

[103] Dowling.

[104] H. Blaxland, "Copy of Letter to Mrs Tilden," in *Blaxland family papers, 1837-1923* (Manuscripts, Oral History & Pictures, State Library of New South Wales, Sydney, Catalogue Ab50, 1829).

[105] The Sydney Morning Herald, "Deaths (George Blaxland)," *The Sydney Morning Herald (NSW: 1842-1954)*, Thursday 11 October 1855 1855.

[106] "Mails by the European and Australian Royal Mail Company's Steamer Oneida," *The Sydney Morning Herald (NSW: 1842-1954)*, Thursday 22 January 1857.

[107] For an overview of the Bengal Mutiny, see Part 4 in L. James, *Raj: The Making and Unmaking of British India* (New York, NY: St Martin's Press, 1998).

[108] The Sydney Morning Herald, "The Wrecked P. and O. Company's Steamer Ava (from the Ceylon Observer)," *The Sydney Morning Herald (NSW: 1842-1954)*, Saturday 1st May 1858.

[109] Her Britannic Majesty's Consul, "Passport Issued by John Green, Her Britannic Majesty's Consul at Alexandria in Egypt, to Lady Harriet Dowling, Her Granddaughter Kate Macdonald Ritchie, and a Female Servant Named Elizabeth Hill, in Order to Travel to England Via the Continent, 19 March 1858," (Manuscripts, Oral History & Pictures, State Library of New South Wales, State Library of NSW, Catalogue Ad60, 1858).

[110] Ibid.

[111] The Sydney Morning Herald, "From the Home News: Female Emigration to Australia," *Sydney Morning Herald (NSW: 1842-1954)*, Tuesday 27 January 1863.

[112] Australian Town and Country Journal, "Shipping Arrivals, December 28," *Australian Town and Country Journal (NSW, 1870-1907)*, Saturday 30 December 1871.

[113] Morris, pp. 29, 33.

[114] A.R. Dowling, "Dowling, James Sheen (1819-1902)," National Centre of Biography, Australian National University, http://adb.anu.edu.au/biography/dowling-james-sheen-3436, published first in hardcopy 1972, online access confirmed 1 February 2017.

[115] The Sydney Morning Herald, "Death of Mr Vincent Dowling," *The Sydney Morning Herald (NSW: 1842-1954)*, Thursday 25 December 1902.

[116] Obituaries Australia, "Hodgson, Lady Eliza (1821-1902)," National Centre of Biography, Australian National University,

http://oa.anu.edu.au/obituary/hodgson-lady-eliza-1154, online access confirmed 1 February 2017.

[117] Ipswich Herald and General Advertiser, "Queensland News (by Electric Telegraph; from Our Correspondent)," *Ipswich Herald and General Advertiser (QLD: 1861-1908)*, Tuesday 18 October 1898.

[118] The Sydney Morning Herald, "Advertising: Wanted," *Sydney Morning Herald (NSW: 1842-1954)*, Wednesday 17 January 1872.

[119] The Sydney Mail and New South Wales Advertiser, "Anglican Church Conference: Picnic to Lithgow Valley," *The Sydney Mail and New South Wales Advertiser (NSW: 1871-1912)*, Saturday 19 October 1872.

[120] The Sydney Morning Herald, "Advertising: Wanted," *Sydney Morning Herald (NSW: 1842-1954)*, Thursday 19 June 1873.

[121] "Advertising: Public Auction," *Sydney Morning Herald (NSW: 1842-1954)*, Friday 8 August 1873.

[122] "One of Claxton's Pictures," *Sydney Morning Herald (NSW: 1842-1954)*, Thursday 14 August 1873.

[123] "List of Donations to the Australian Museum During August and September 1873," *Sydney Morning Herald (NSW: 1842-1954)*, Monday 6 October 1873.

[124] "Royal Mail Notice," *Sydney Morning Herald (NSW: 1842-1954)*, Tuesday 2 December 1873.

[125] Launceston Examiner, "Deaths: Arthur Macdonald Ritchie," *Launceston Examiner (Tas: 1842-1899)*, Saturday 31 August 1878.

[126] The Sydney Morning Herald, "News of the Day (Lady Dowling's Death)," *Sydney Morning Herald (NSW: 1842-1954)*, Saturday 21 May 1881.

[127] Goulburn Herald, "(Lady Dowling's Death)," *Goulburn Herald (NSW 1881-1907)* 1881.

[128] The Sydney Morning Herald, "Deaths (Louisa Australia Blaxland)," *The Sydney Morning Herald (NSW: 1842-1954)*, Saturday 4 August 1888.

[129] The Sydney Gazette and New South Wales Advertiser, "Ship News," *The Sydney Gazette and New South Wales Advertiser (NSW: 1803 - 1842)*, Sunday 5 April 1807.

[130] Kercher, p. 157.

[131] S. Weintraub, "The King's Loose Box: Edward VII as Priapic Prince of Wales," *English Literature in Transition* 60, no. 1 (2017).

Index

A

aboriginal population 8
agency house (of East India Company) 33, 40
Andrews (Hogue), Elizabeth (aunt) 12–14, 19, 81
ayah 16, 19, 28, 29, 31, 41

B

Blaxland (Breton), Eliza Maria 7, 45, 80
Blaxland (Molle), Mary Ellen 45, 62, 80
Blaxland (Ritchie, Dowling), Harriet Mary
    adolescence *9–15*
    bankrupt *39–42*
    childhood *2–9*
    flirtation *34–38*
    in Agra *28–32*
    in Kolkata *16–25*
    marriage to Dowling *54–63*
    marriage to Ritchie *24–44*

Blaxland (Walker), Anna Elizabeth . 7, 11, 33, 45, 55, 60, 62, 65, 71, 78, 80
Blaxland, Arthur 45, 65–66, 76, 80
Blaxland, Edward 17, 45, 65–66, 73, 76, 78, 80
Blaxland, George ... 7, 14–16, 17–18, 21, 33, 45, 49–50, 54, 61, 64–65, 70, 72, 76, 80
Blaxland, Gregory 3–4, 10, 12
Blaxland, Harriet Mary (mother) .. See *de Marquet (Blaxland), Harriet Mary*
Blaxland, Jane Elizabeth 7, 11, 45, 49, 50–53, 60, 62, 80
Blaxland, John (father) 2–7, 9–11, 13–14, 26, 33–34, 46–49, 50, 55, 81
Blaxland, John Marquet (brother) 7, 45, 61, 80
Blaxland, Louisa Australia 2, 7, 11, 36, 45, 49, 51, 64–65, 71, 76, 78, 80
Blaxland, Maria .... See *Dowling (Blaxland), Maria*
Bligh (Putland, O'Connell), Mary 58–59
Bligh, William 5–7, 10, 58
Bougainville, Hyacinthe 34–38
Boydell, Charles 59, 76, 82
Boydell, Elizabeth ('Eliza') .... See *Ritchie (Boydell), Elizabeth ('Eliza')*
Breton, Eliza Maria .... See *Blaxland (Breton), Eliza Maria*
Breton, Henry W. 51, 80
Brougham Lodge, Darlinghurst 55–56, 72
Brush Farm 4
Burton, William 57, 62–63

C

cholera 26–28
convicts 3, 5, 8, 34, 57, 62, 66, 70
Cowin, Captain 11–12, 14

D

dacoits 29
de Marquet (Blaxland), Harriet Mary .. 2, 7, 12–14, 31, 45, 64, 70–72, 81

de Marquet, Louis (John) 13, 81
Dowling (Blaxland), Maria 49–50, 54
Dowling (Hodgson), Eliza 56, 61, 76, 83
Dowling (Spencer), Susannah 56, 61, 76, 83
Dowling, Anne 56, 83
Dowling, Harriet Mary .... **See** *Blaxland (Ritchie, Dowling), Harriet Mary*
Dowling, James (second husband) .. 49–50, 52–54, 55–63, 66, 71, 80, 83
Dowling, James Sheen (step-son) 50, 56–57, 59, 76, 83
Dowling, Vincent (brother-in-law) 69
Dowling, Vincent Francis Woodcock 55, 61, 72, 76, 83

E

East India Company (British) 13, 20–22, 29, 32, 33, 40

F

Forbes, Amelia S. 57, 66
Forbes, Francis 57
Forster, Thomas 55
Franklin, Jane 44, 58–59

G

Gipps, Elizabeth 44
Gipps, George 57, 62–63

H

Hodgson, Eliza .... **See** *Dowling (Hodgson), Eliza*
Hogue, Arthur (cousin) 61, 81
Hogue, Arthur (uncle) 13–26, 28, 81
Hogue, Davidson and Robertson 13, 21
Hogue, Elizabeth (aunt) .... **See** *Andrews (Hogue), Elizabeth (aunt)*
Hugli River 7, 17, 26

J

Johnston, George 6

L

Lord, Simeon 5–6
Luddenham 11

M

Macarthur, John 6
Macdonald, Alexander ('Sandy') See *Ritchie, Alexander Macdonald ('Sandy')*
Macquarie, Lachlan 11
Marsh, James Milbourne 68–70, 76
Molle, Mary Ellen .... See *Blaxland (Molle), Mary Ellen*

N

Newington estate 4–5, 14, 17, 31, 33, 66, 73
Newington House 45–46, 64, 78

O

Ochterlony, David 31–32
O'Connell, Mary .... See *Bligh (Putland, O'Connell), Mary*

P

Parramatta River 4, 45

R

Rhodes 45, 75
Ritchie (Boydell), Elizabeth ('Eliza') 26, 29, 31, 38, 45, 51, 55, 59, 76, 78
Ritchie, Alexander Macdonald ('Alec' - son). 31, 38, 45, 55, 59, 63, 78, 82
Ritchie, Alexander Macdonald ('Sandy') 22–26, 28–29, 30–32, 33–34, 37–40, 44
Ritchie, Arthur 30–31, 38, 45, 59, 70, 77, 82

Ritchie, Harriet Mary .... *See* Blaxland (Ritchie, Dowling), Harriet Mary

Rum rebellion 6, 58

S

Sati (formerly suttee) 26–27
sepoys 29
servants 8, 17, 19, 20, 29, 34, 40, 43
Sheen (Dowling), Maria 49–50
Ships
    Clonmel 62
    Eliza 15–16
    John Bull 32
    Katherine Stewart Forbes 38
    La Thetis 36
    L'Esperance 36
    Marquis of Lansdowne 41
    Mary Hope 84
    Oneida 73
    Sir George Seymour 84
    The Brothers 3
    Trafalgar 70
    Vimeira 70
    William Young 40
Spencer, Susannah .... *See* Dowling (Spencer), Susannah

T

Taj Mahal, Agra 30
tiger 32

V

von Hügel, Charles 50–53

W

Walker, Anna E. .... *See* Blaxland (Walker), Anna Elizabeth
Walker, Anna Frances 71
Walker, Thomas 33

Z

Zoroastrian 41

www.ingramcontent.com/pod-product-compliance
Lightning Source LLC
Chambersburg PA
CBHW042329150426
43193CB00005B/57